THIS COLORING BOOK BELONGS TO

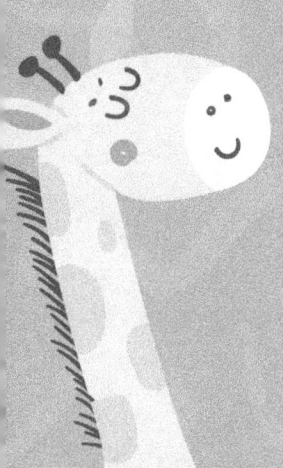

Name : ....

Date : ....

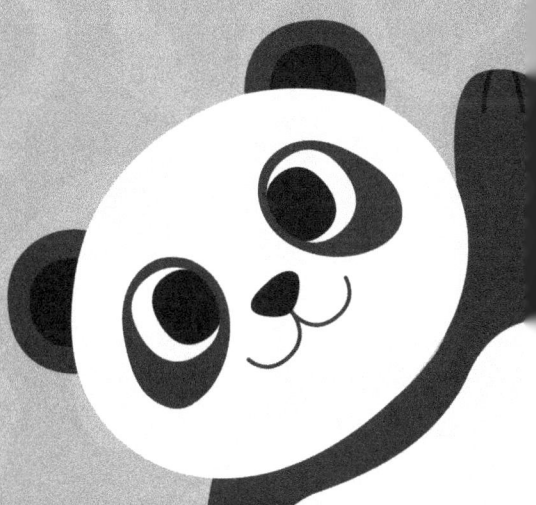

color the rabbits

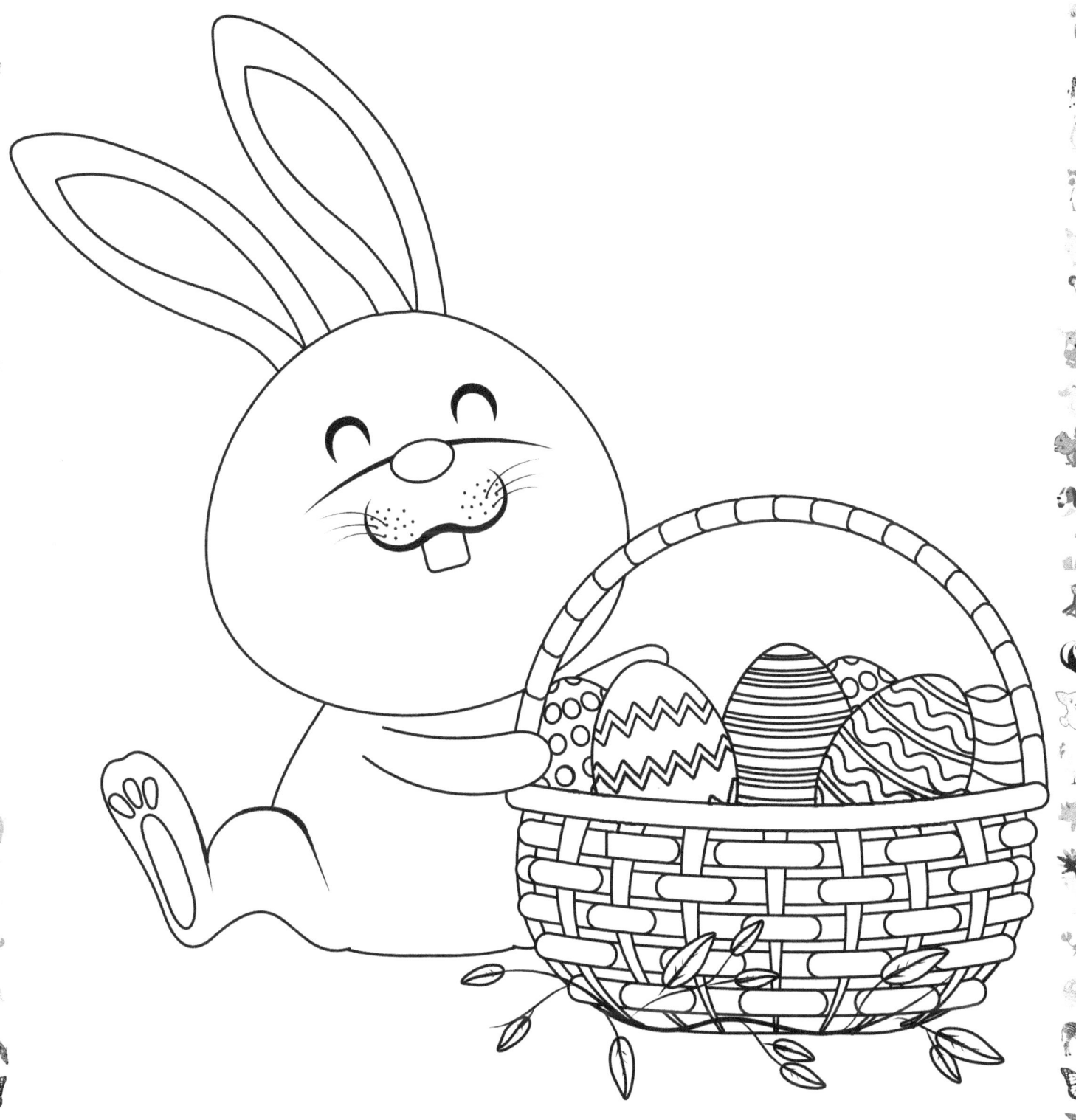

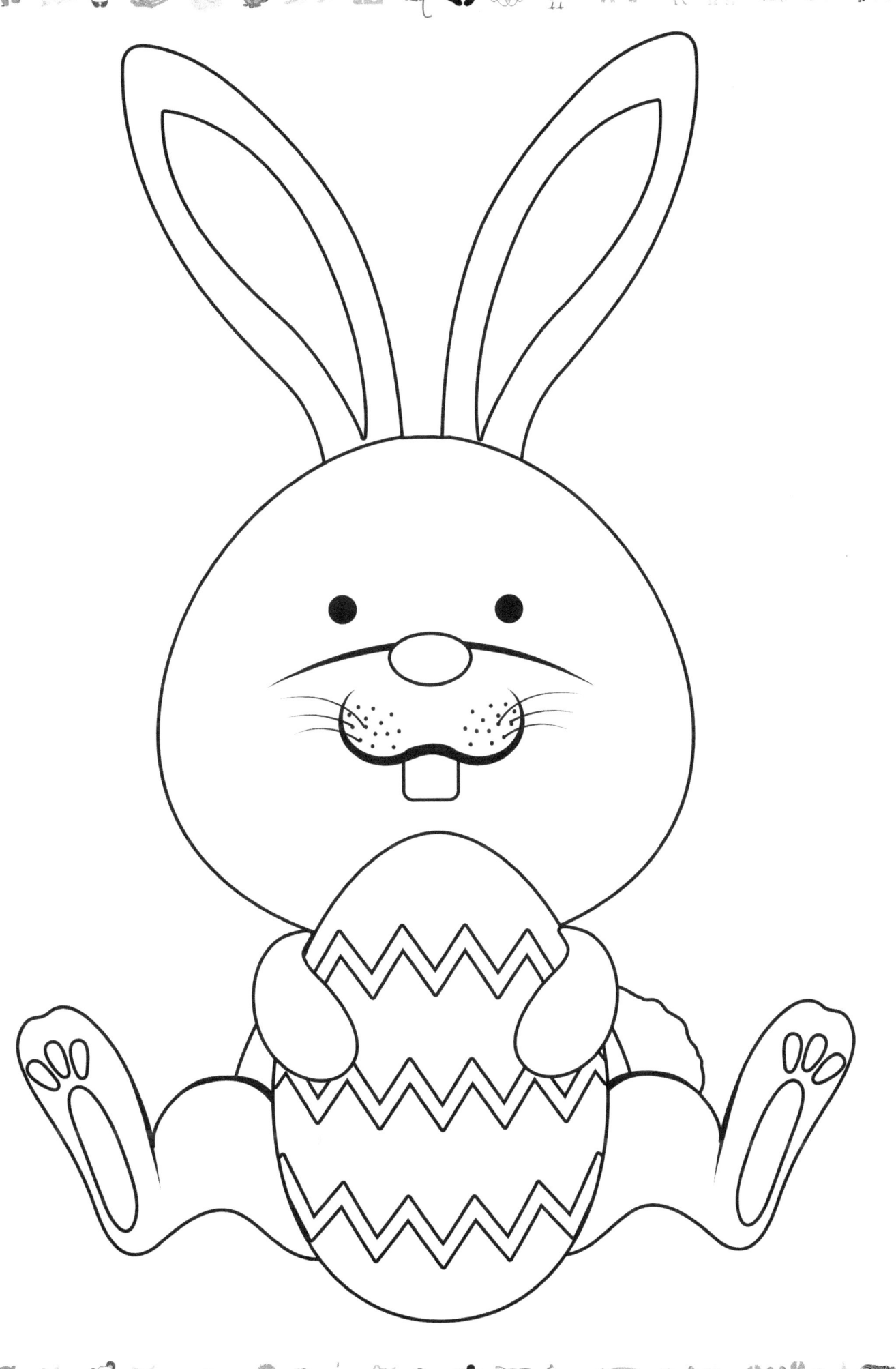

Draw a face on the egg.

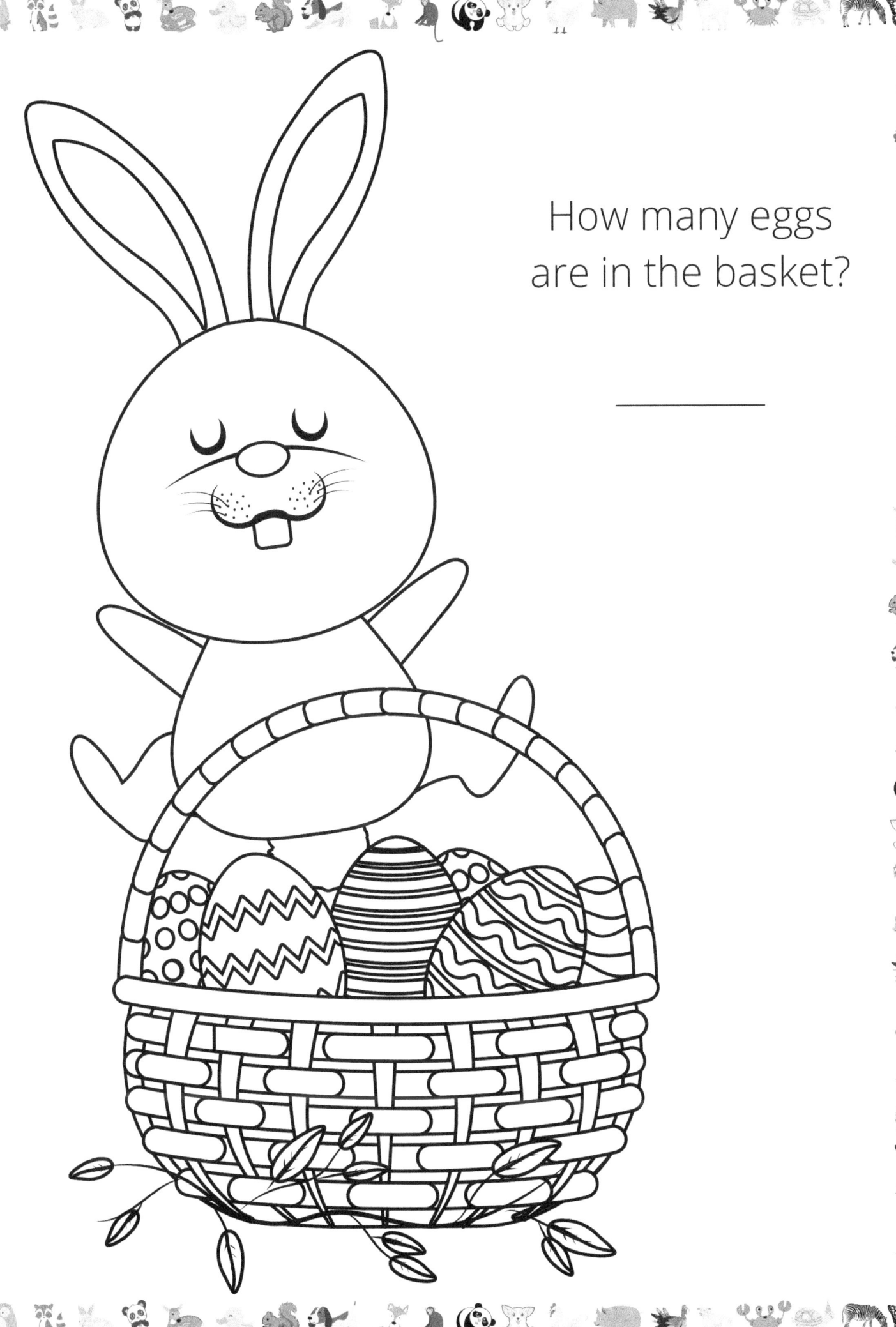

How many eggs
are in the basket?

_____

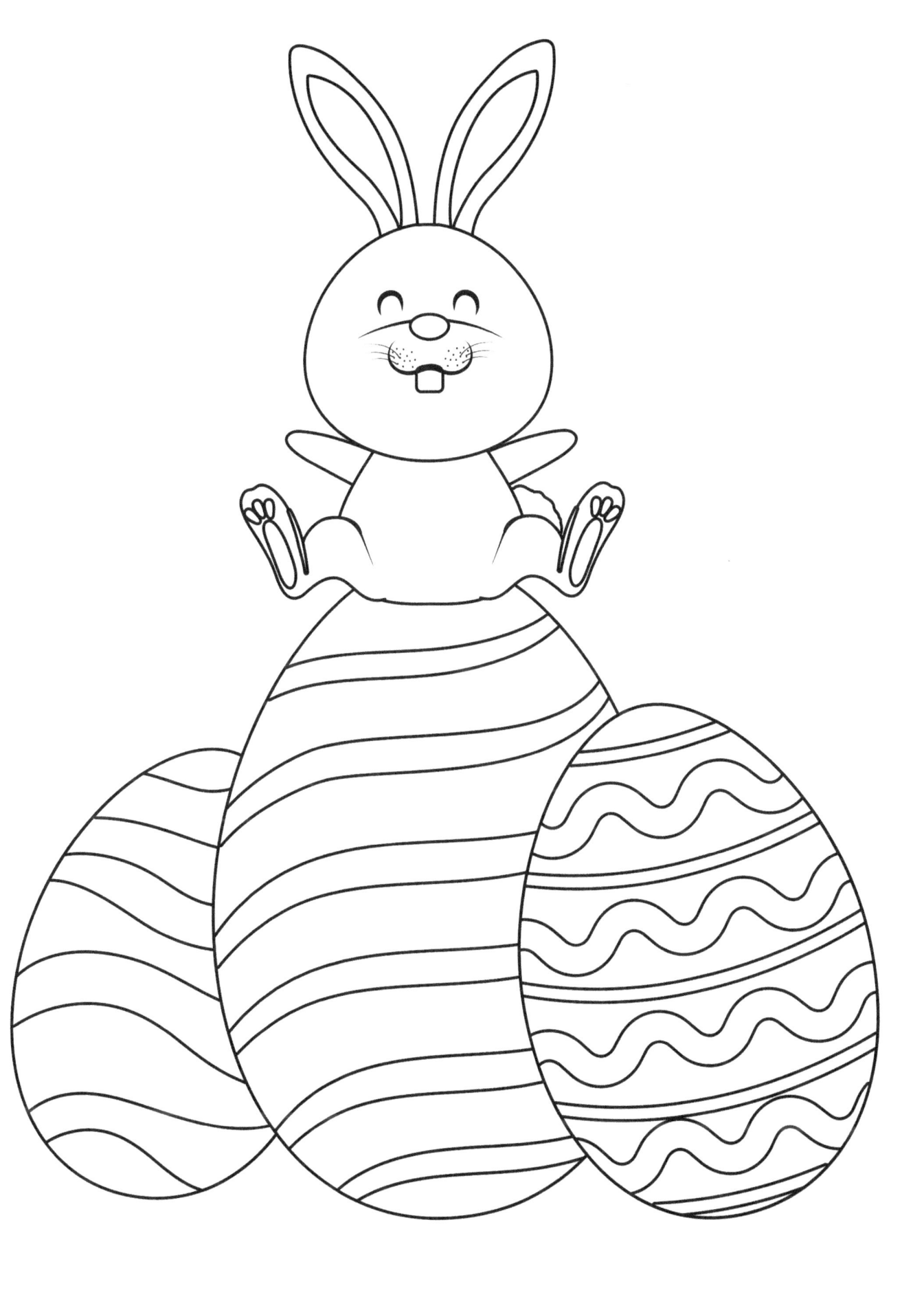

CATS

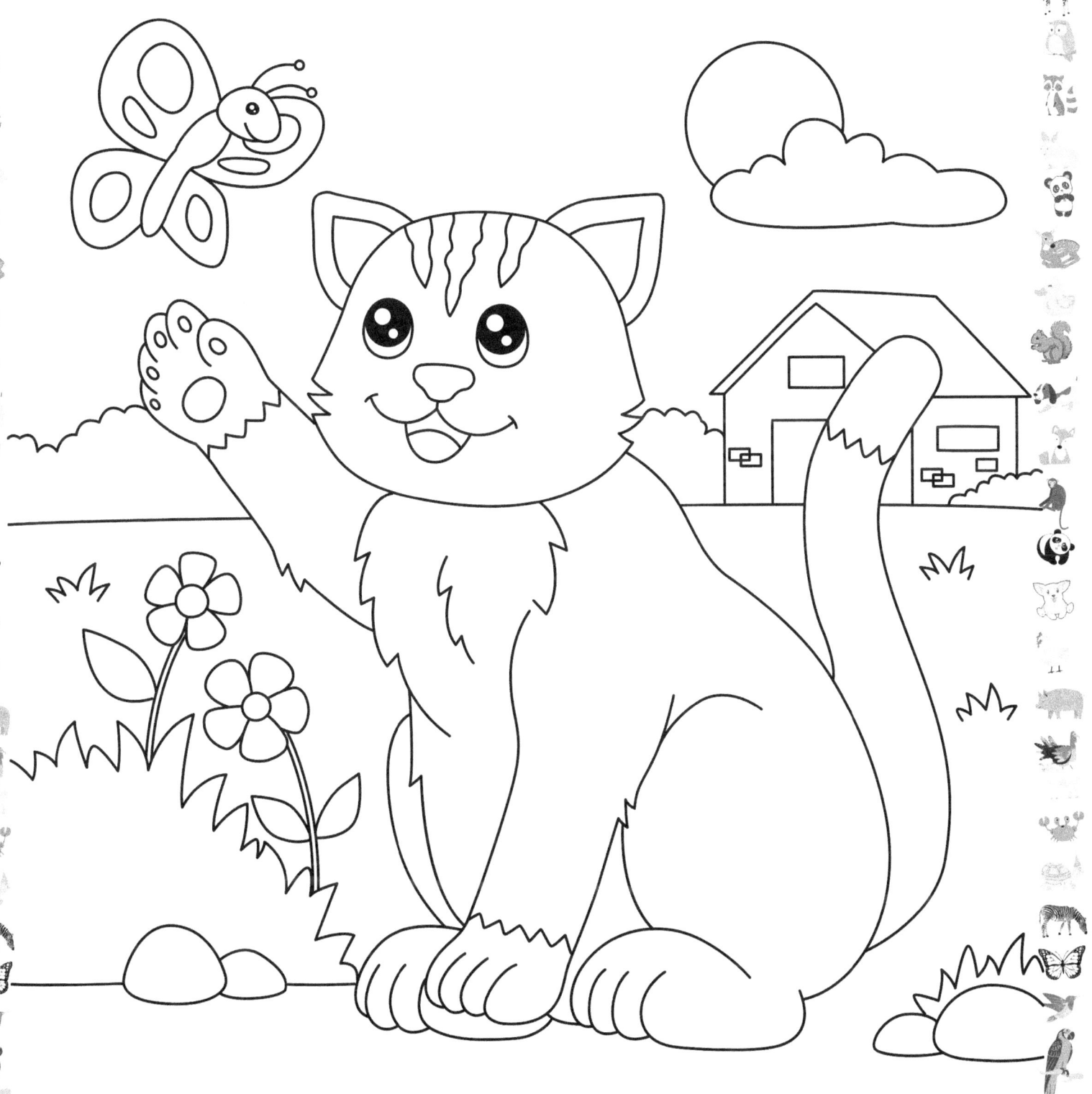

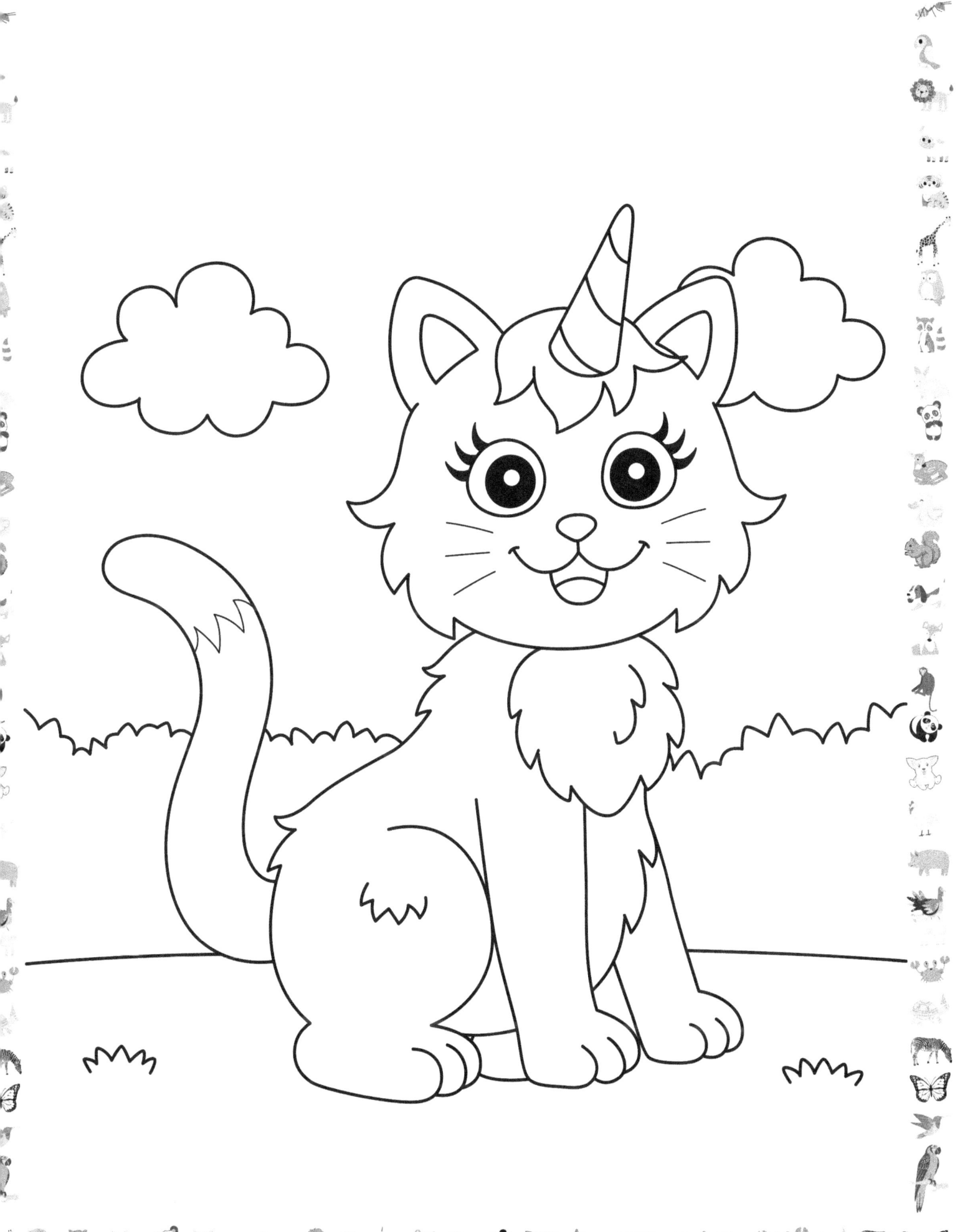

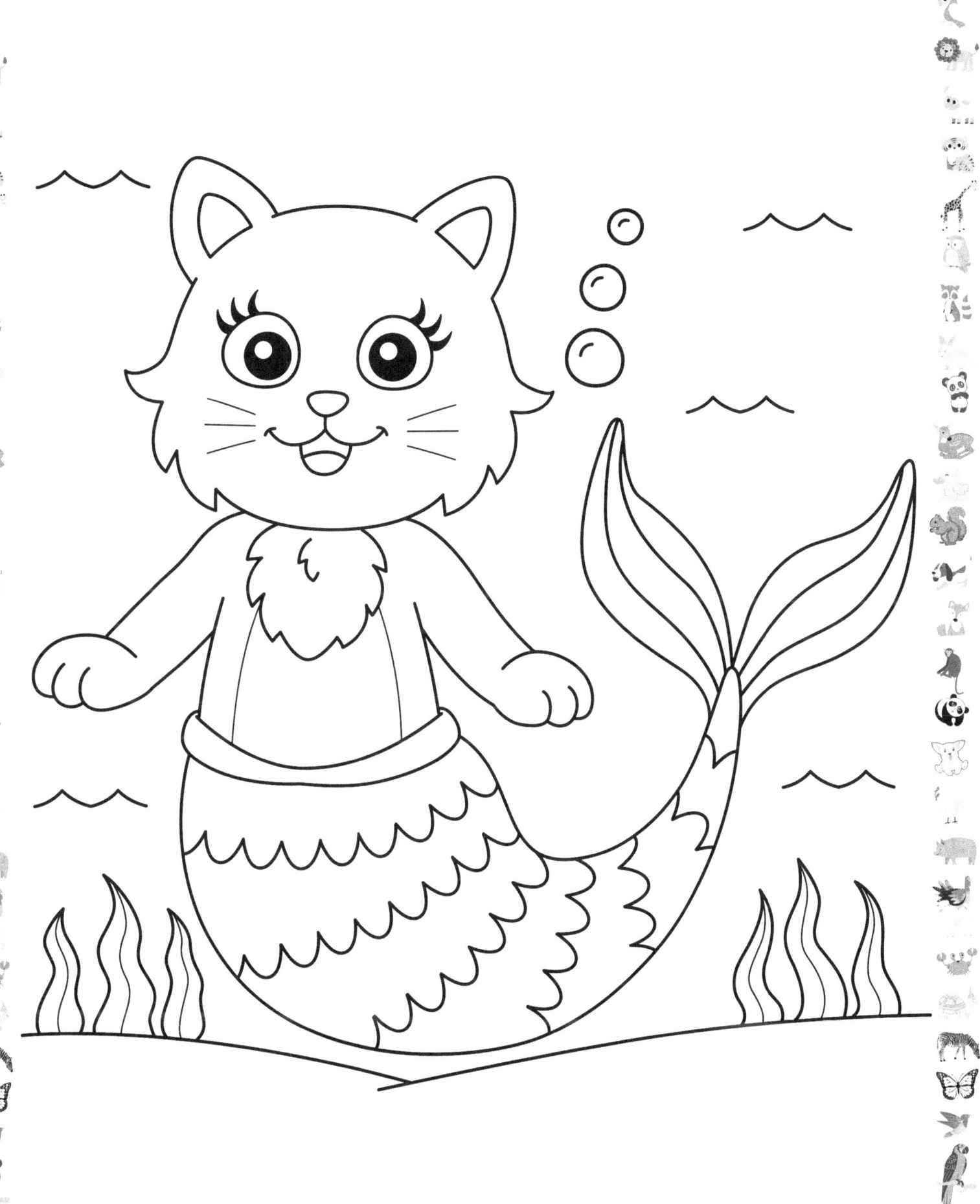

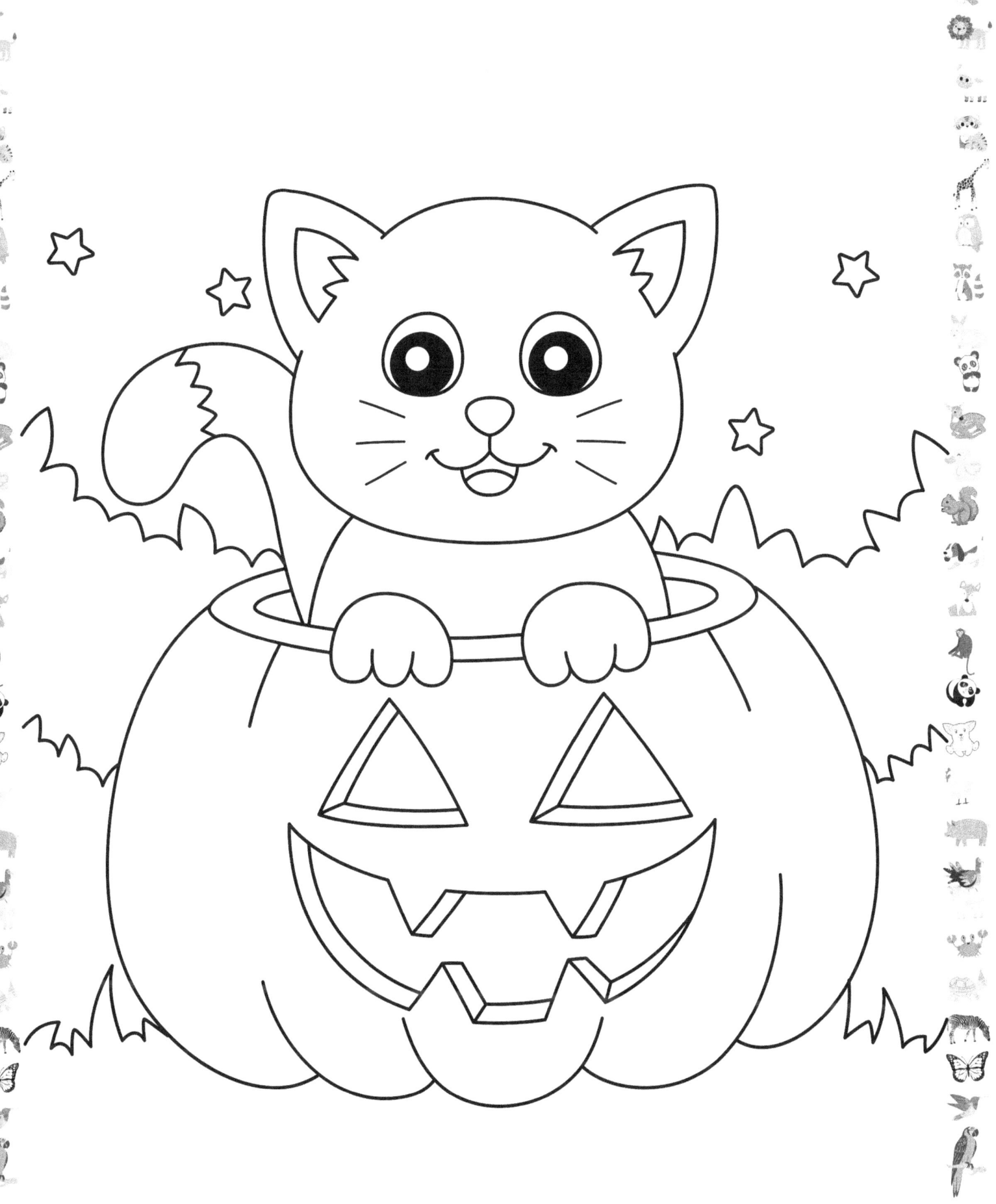

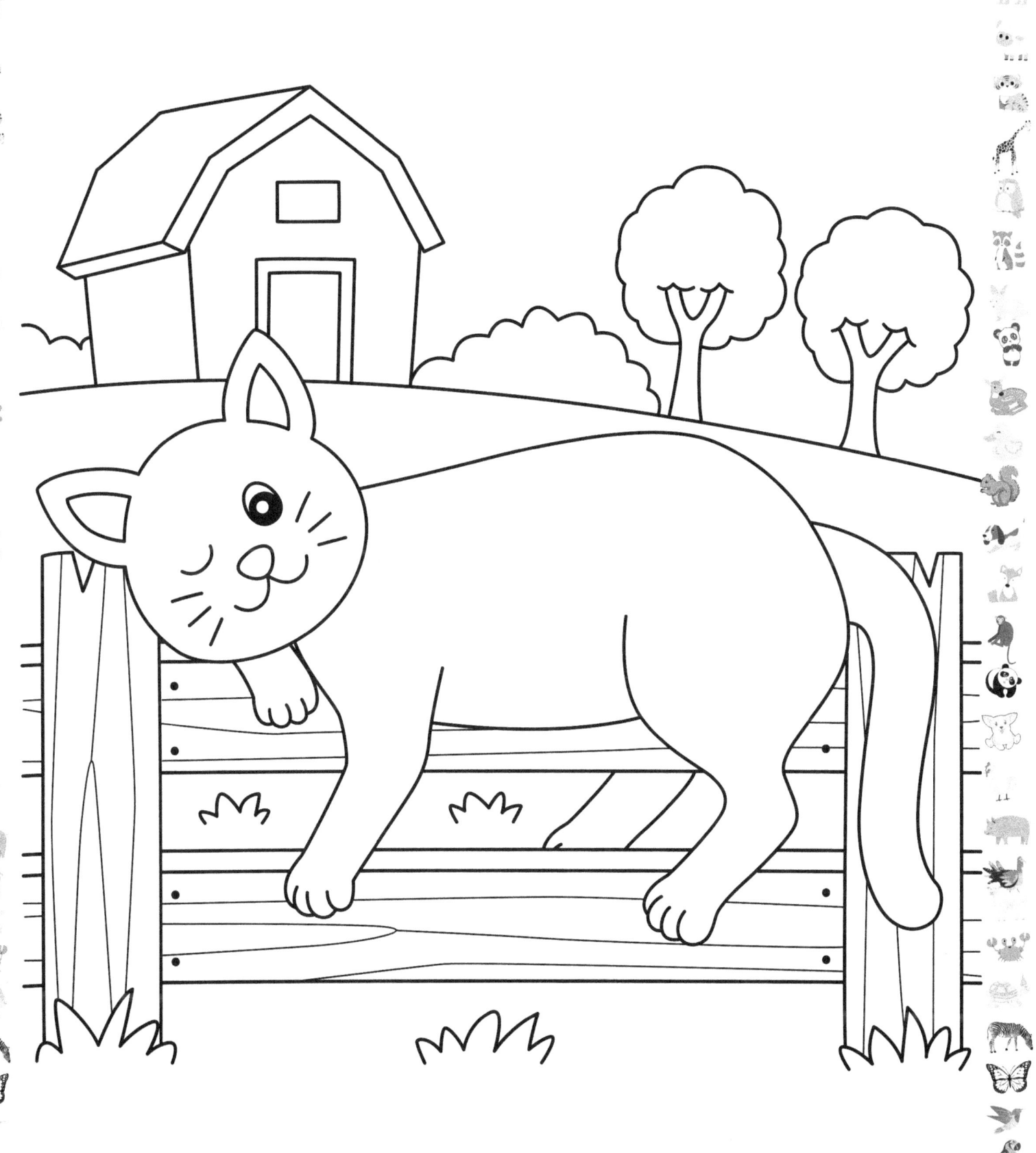

AUSTRALIAN ANIMALS

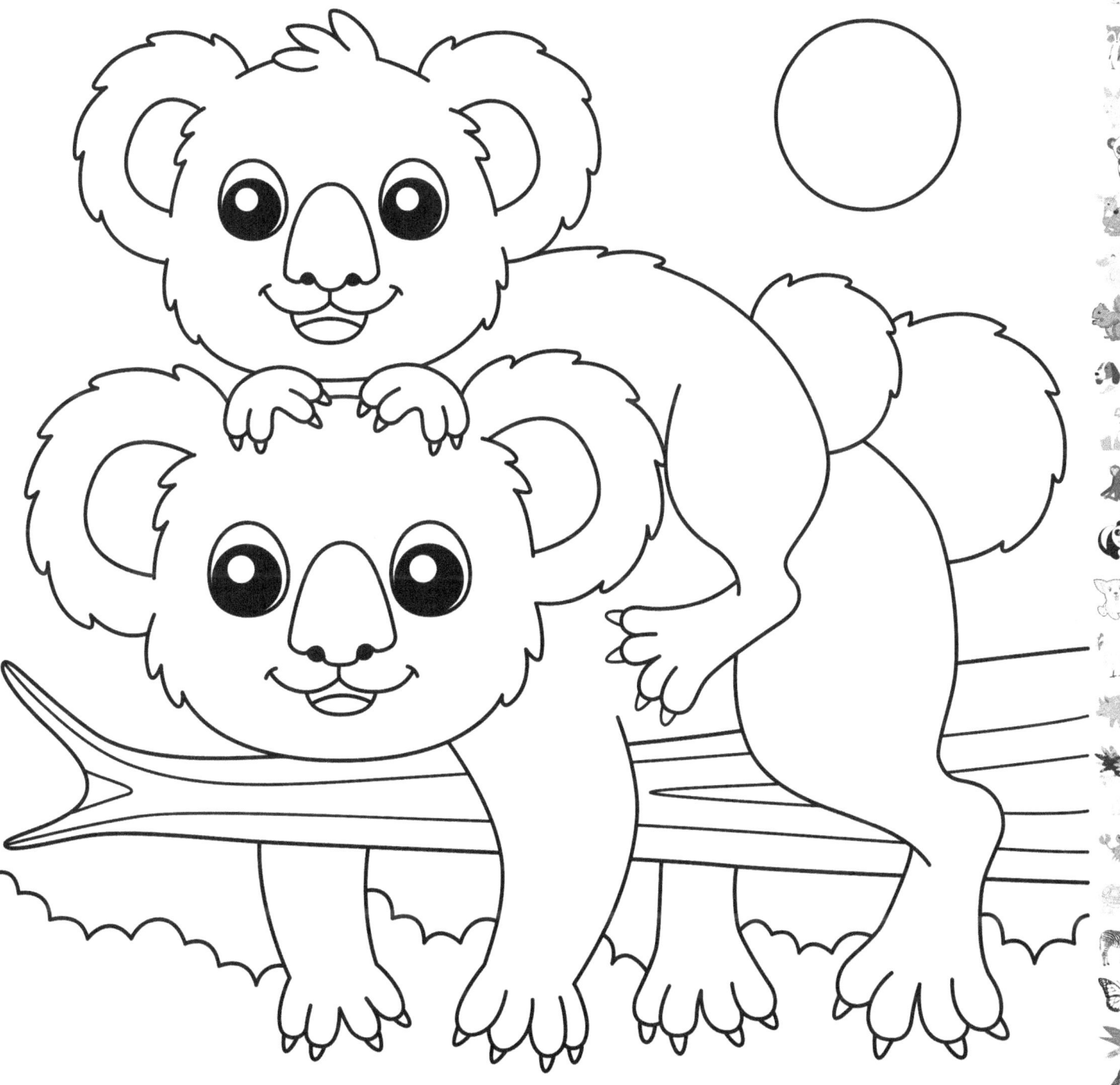

koala

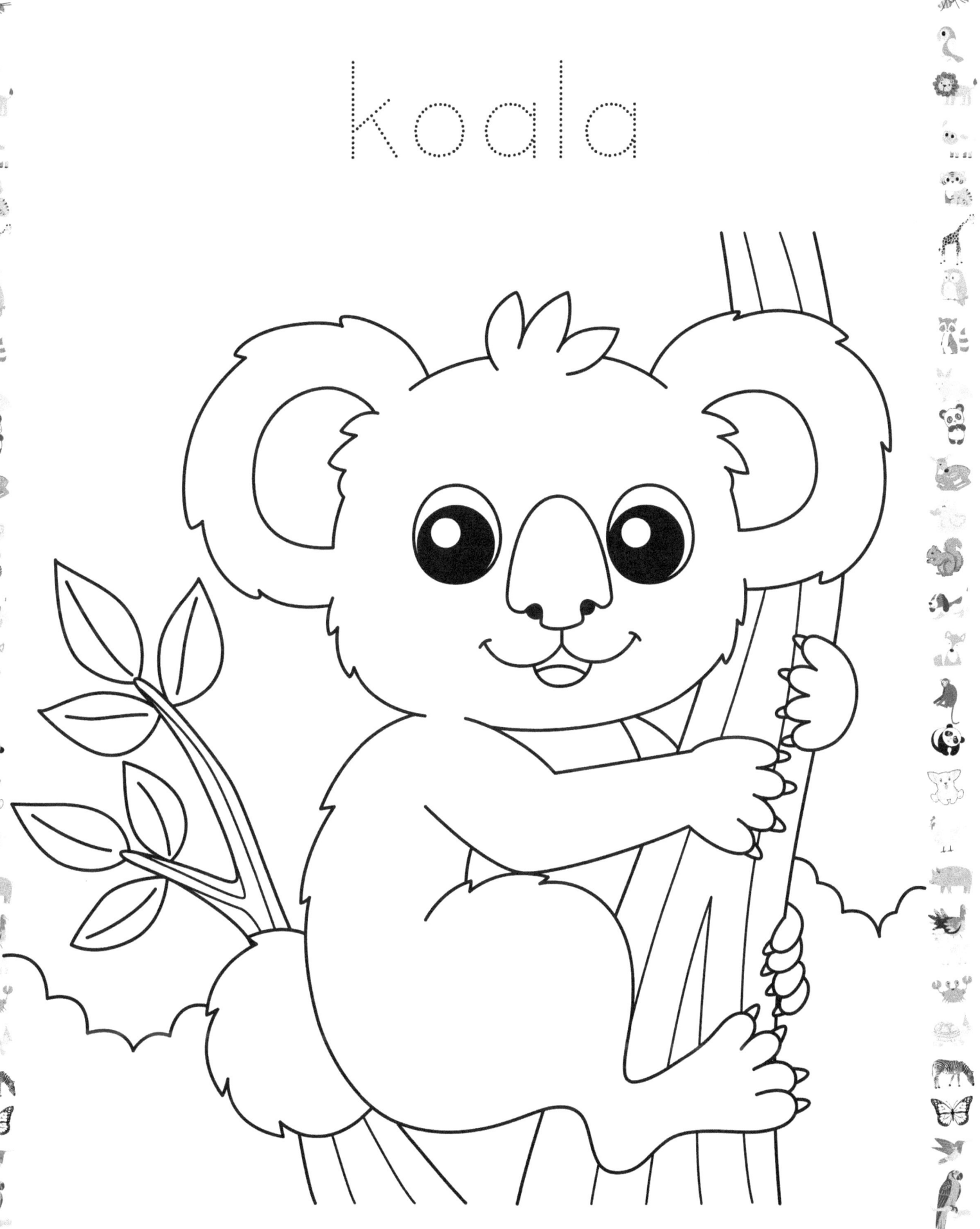

cockatoo

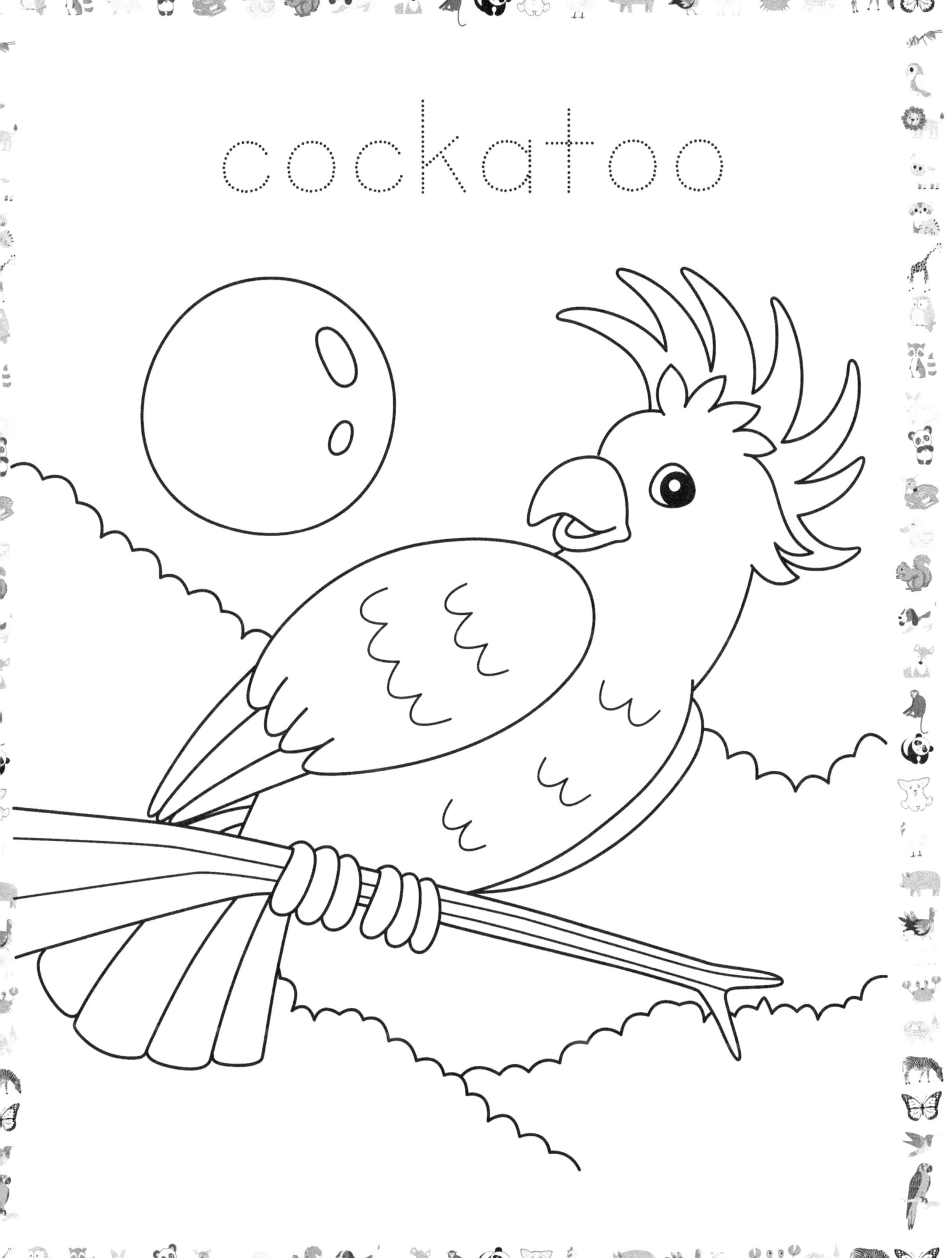

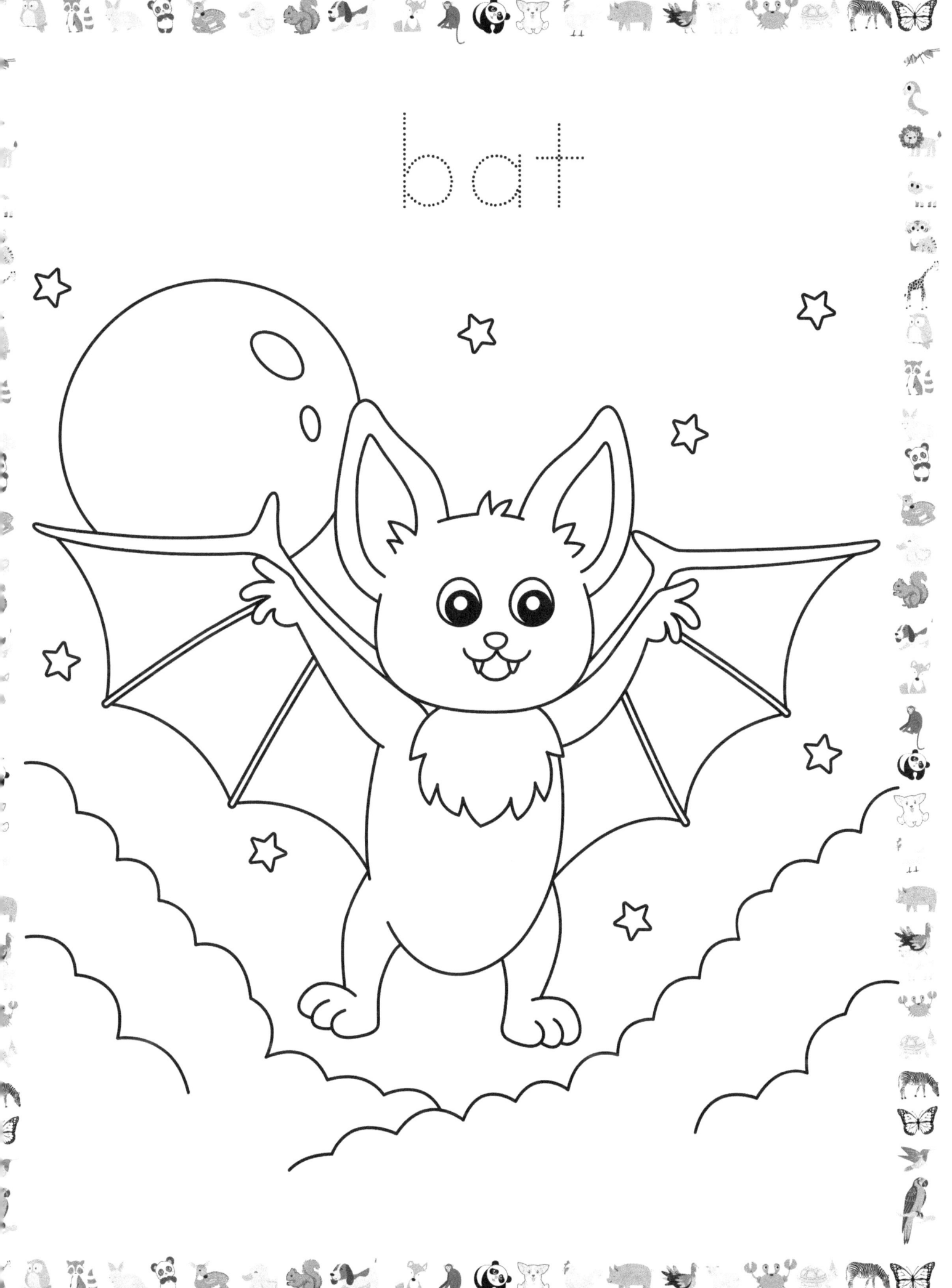

bat

pelican

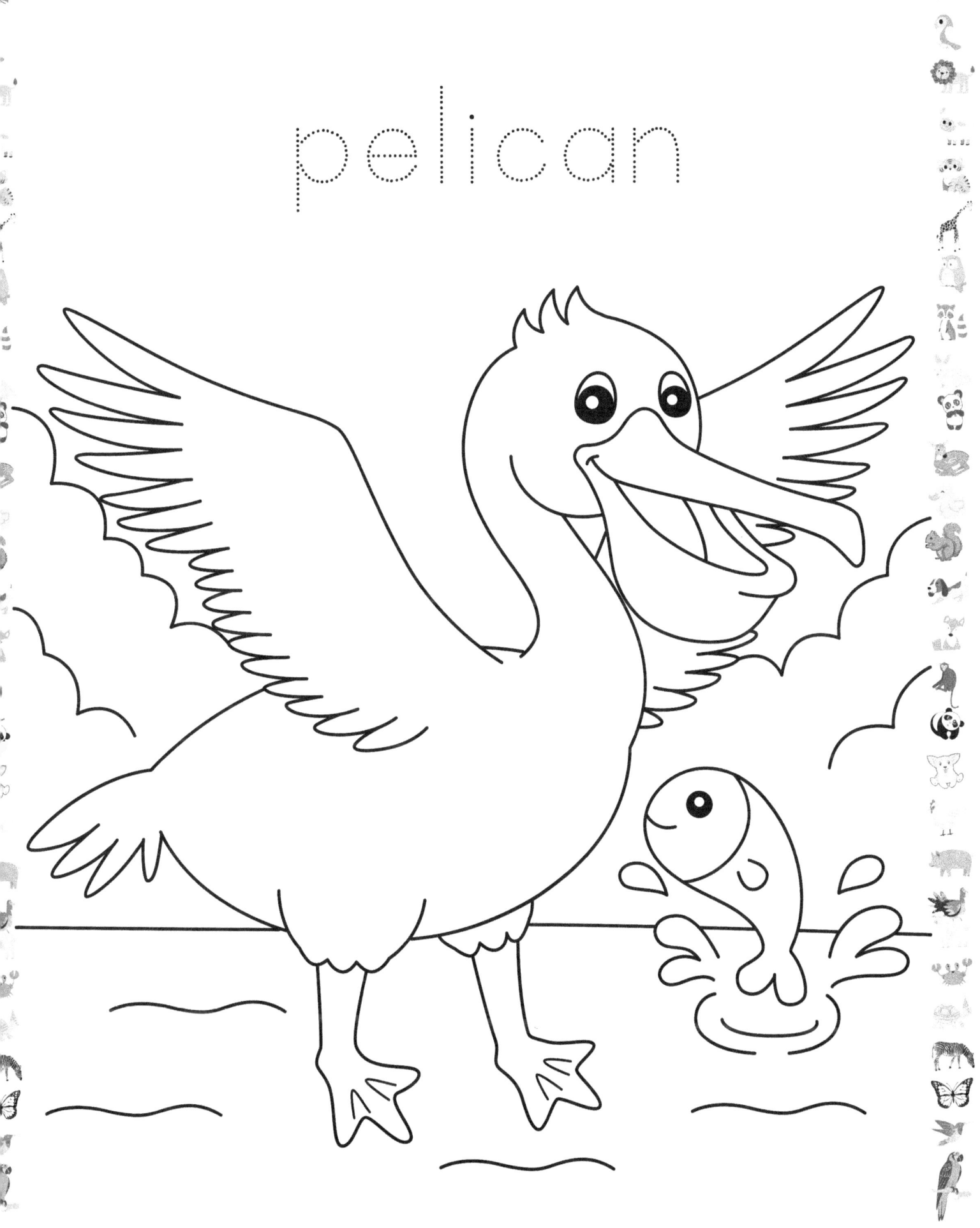

dingo

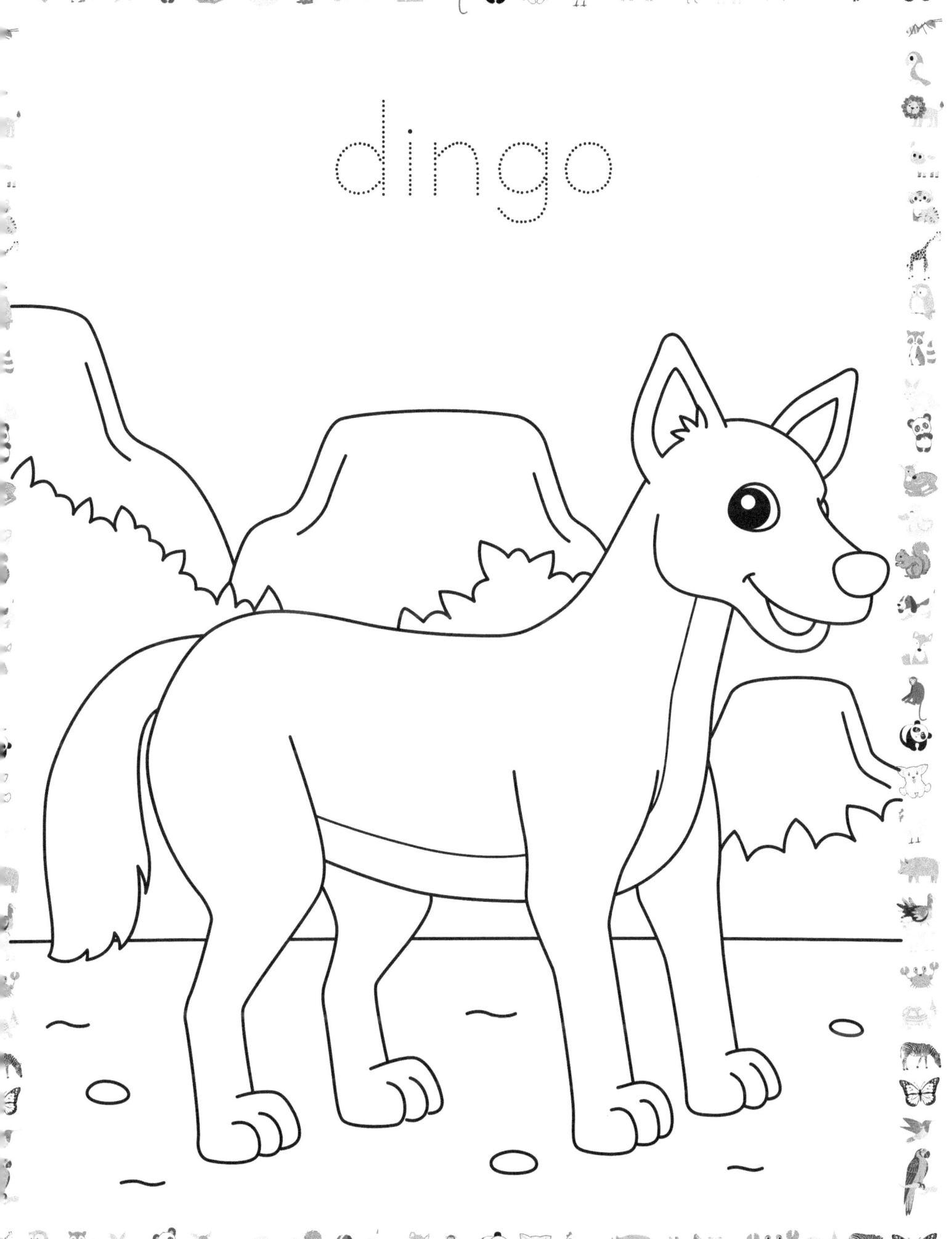

dugong

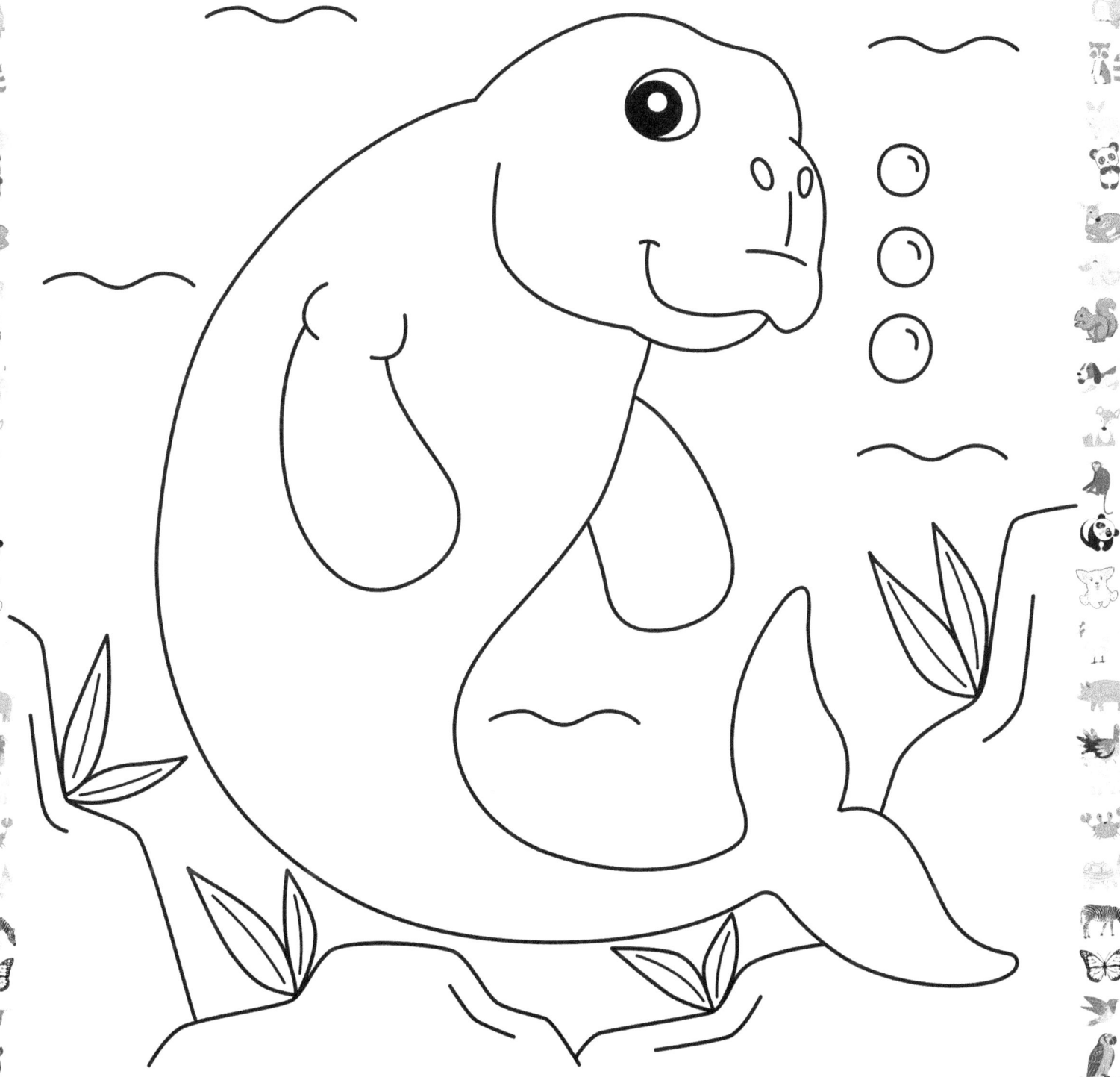

leopard
shark

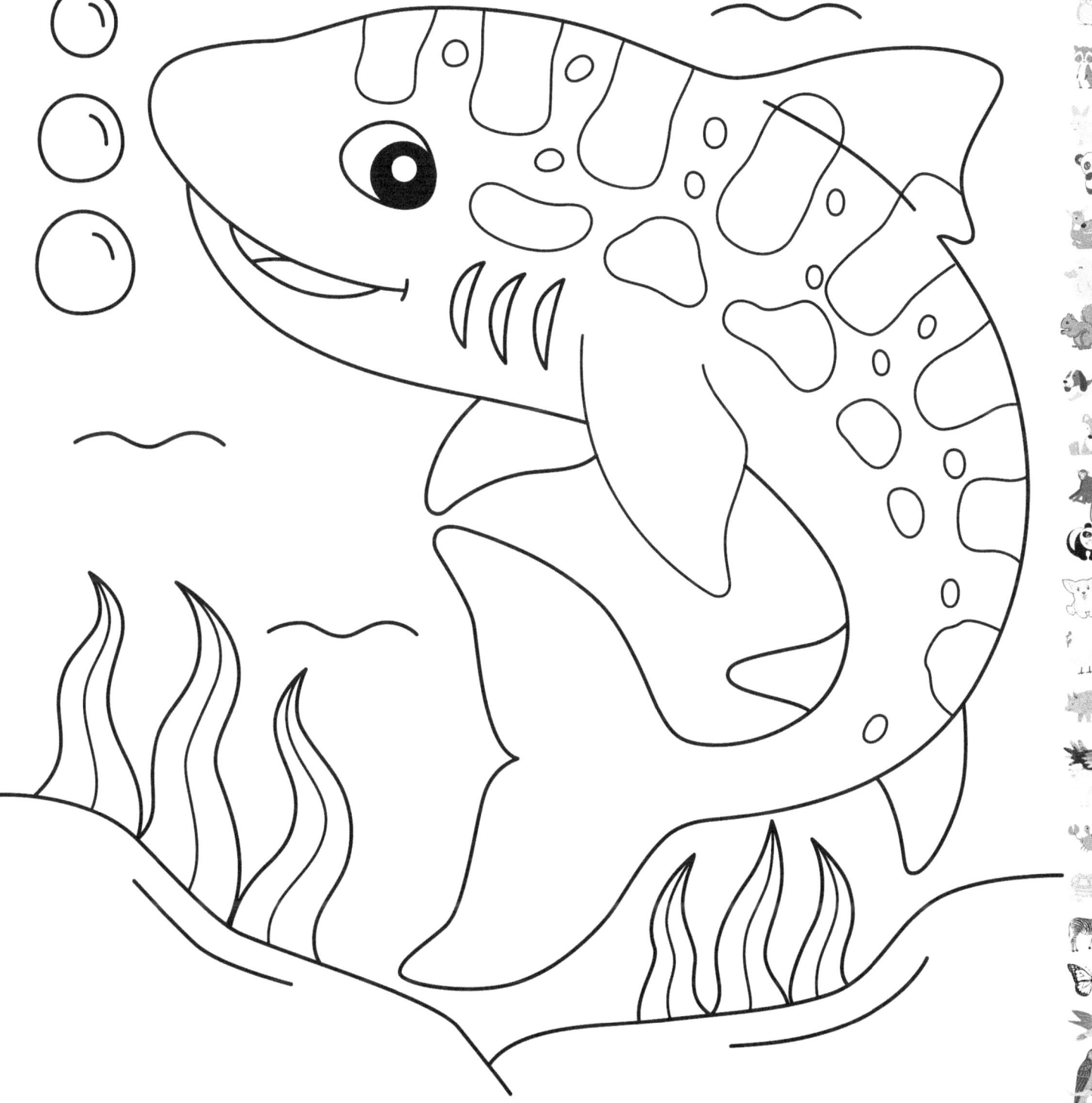

kookaburra

emu

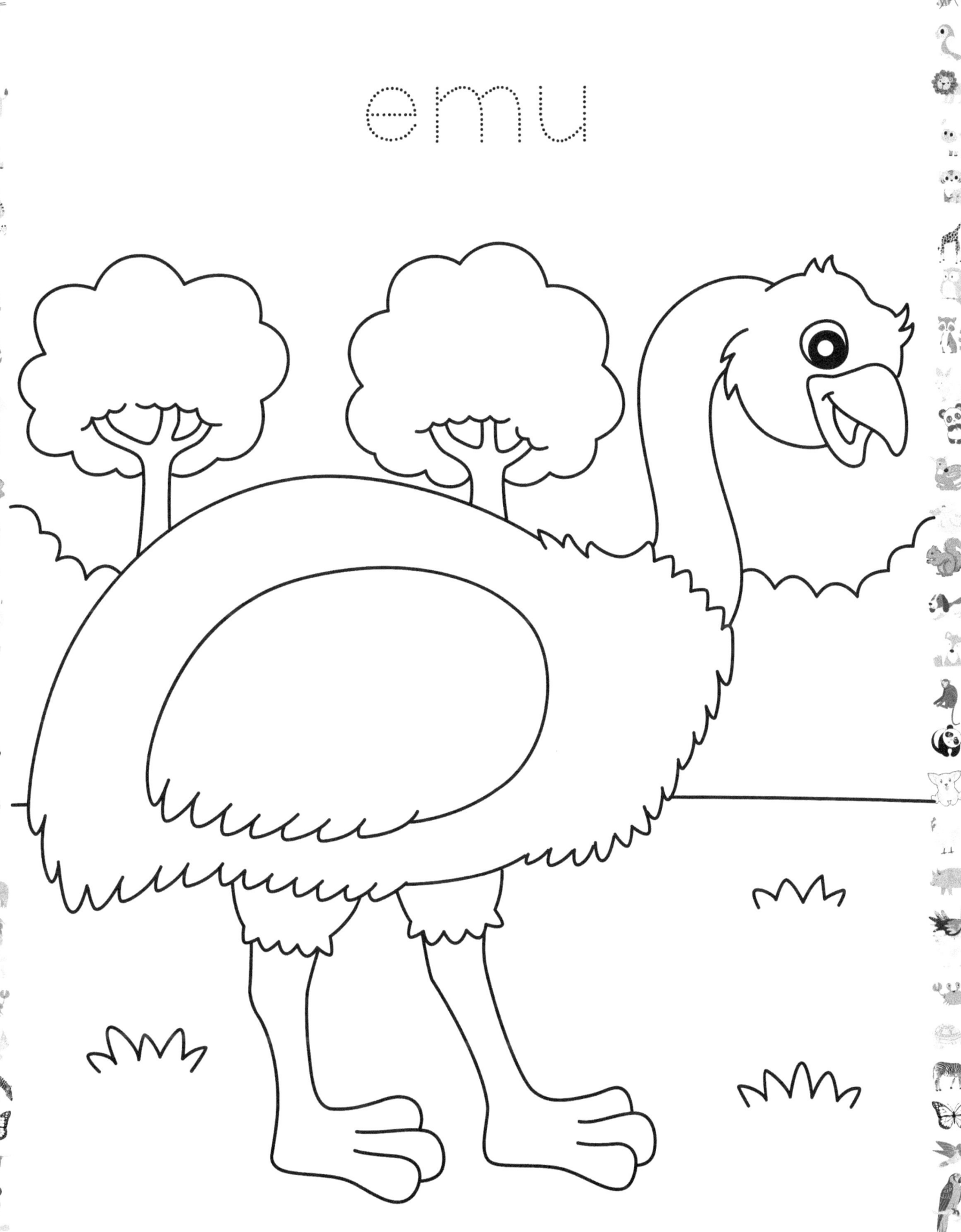

echidna

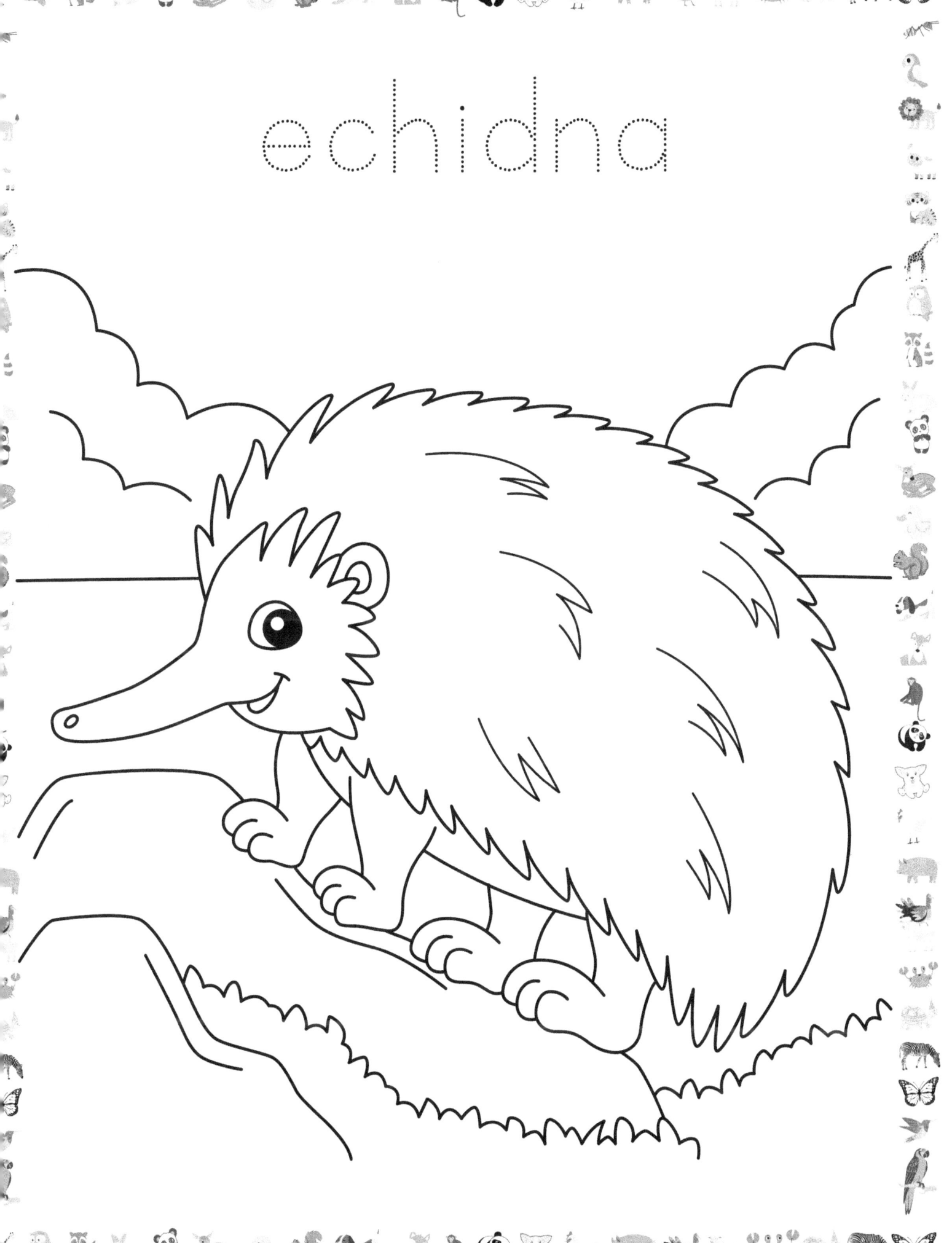

Tasmanian tiger

cassowary

cane toad

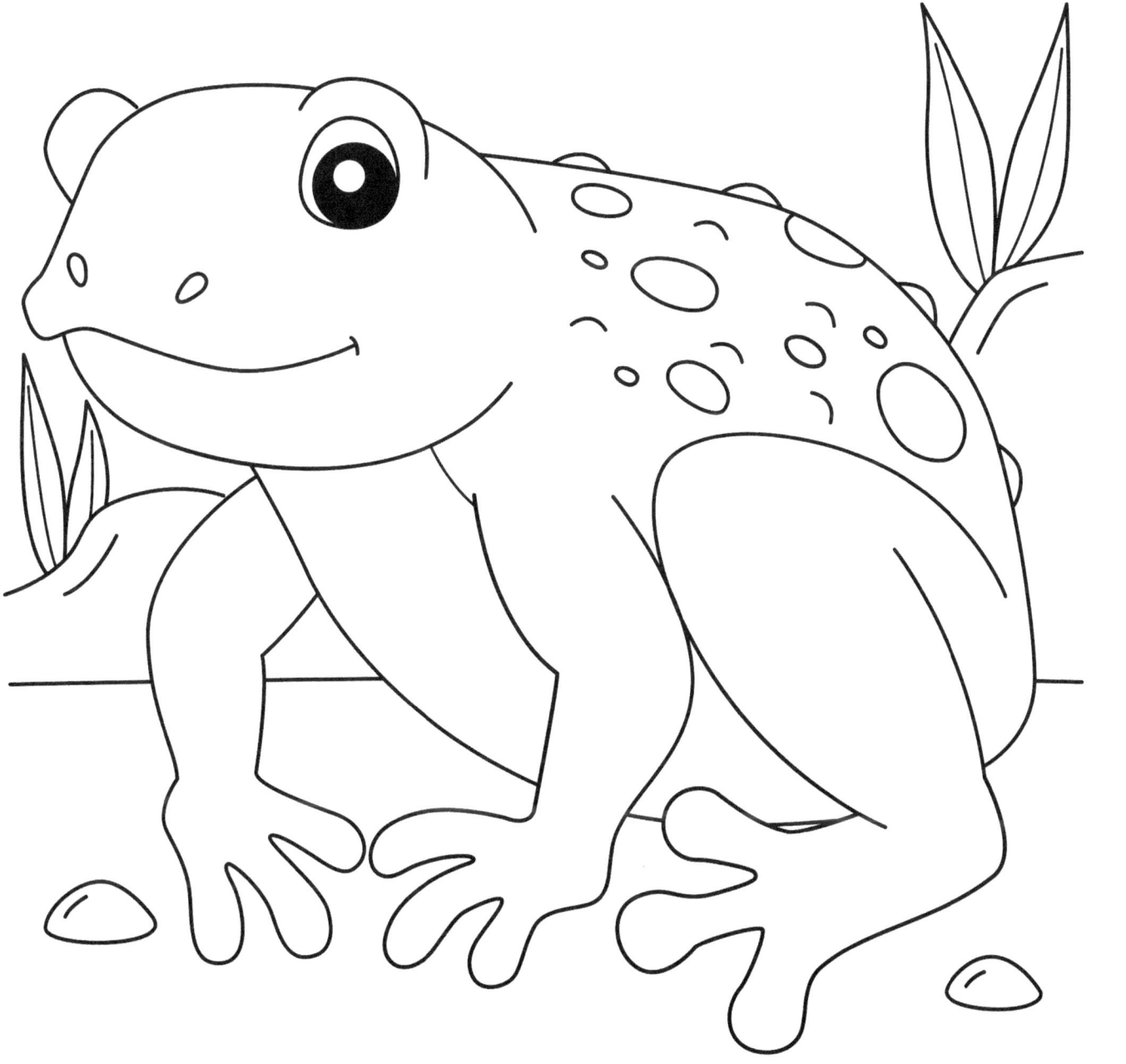

Tasmanian devil

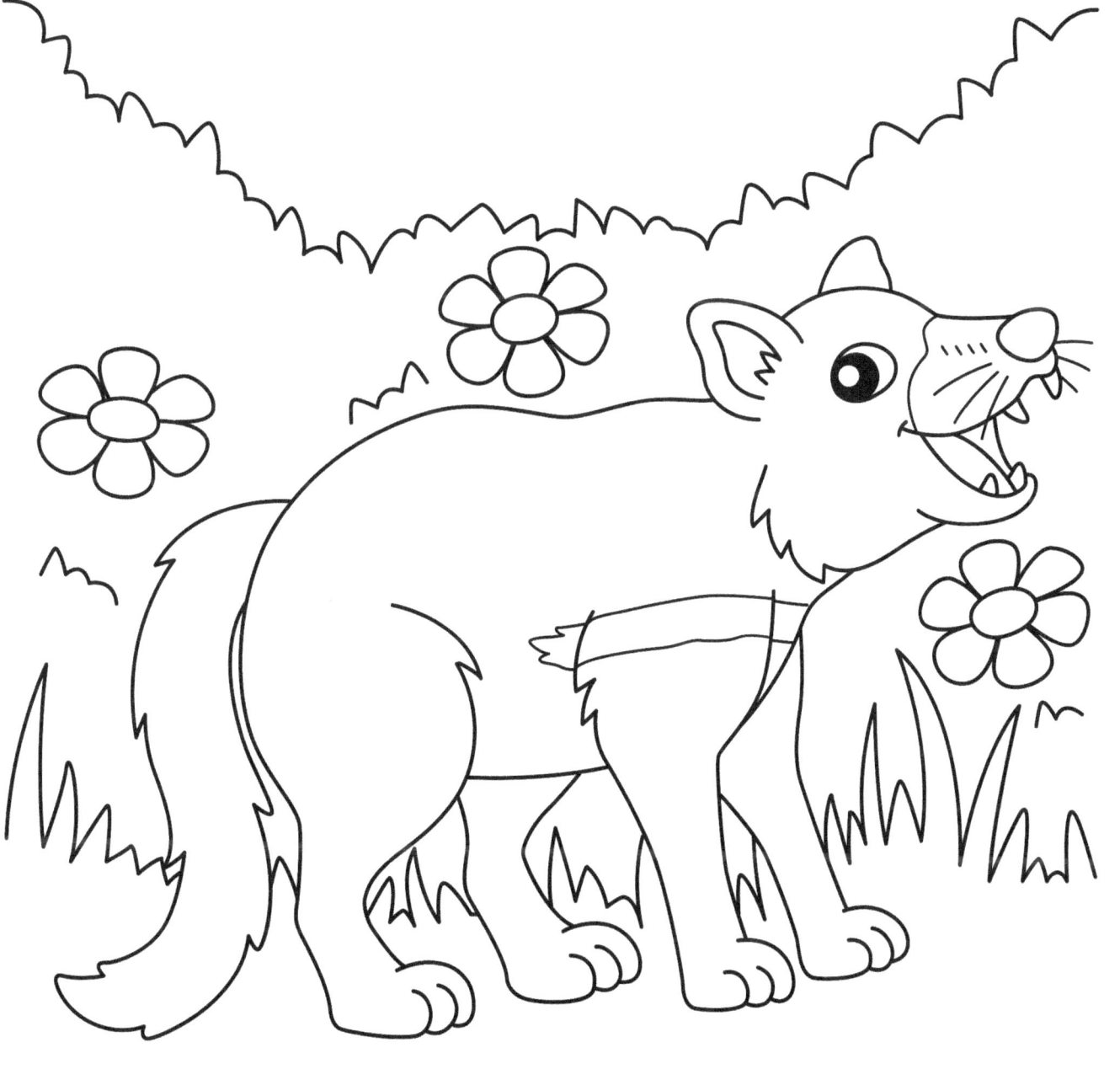

platypus

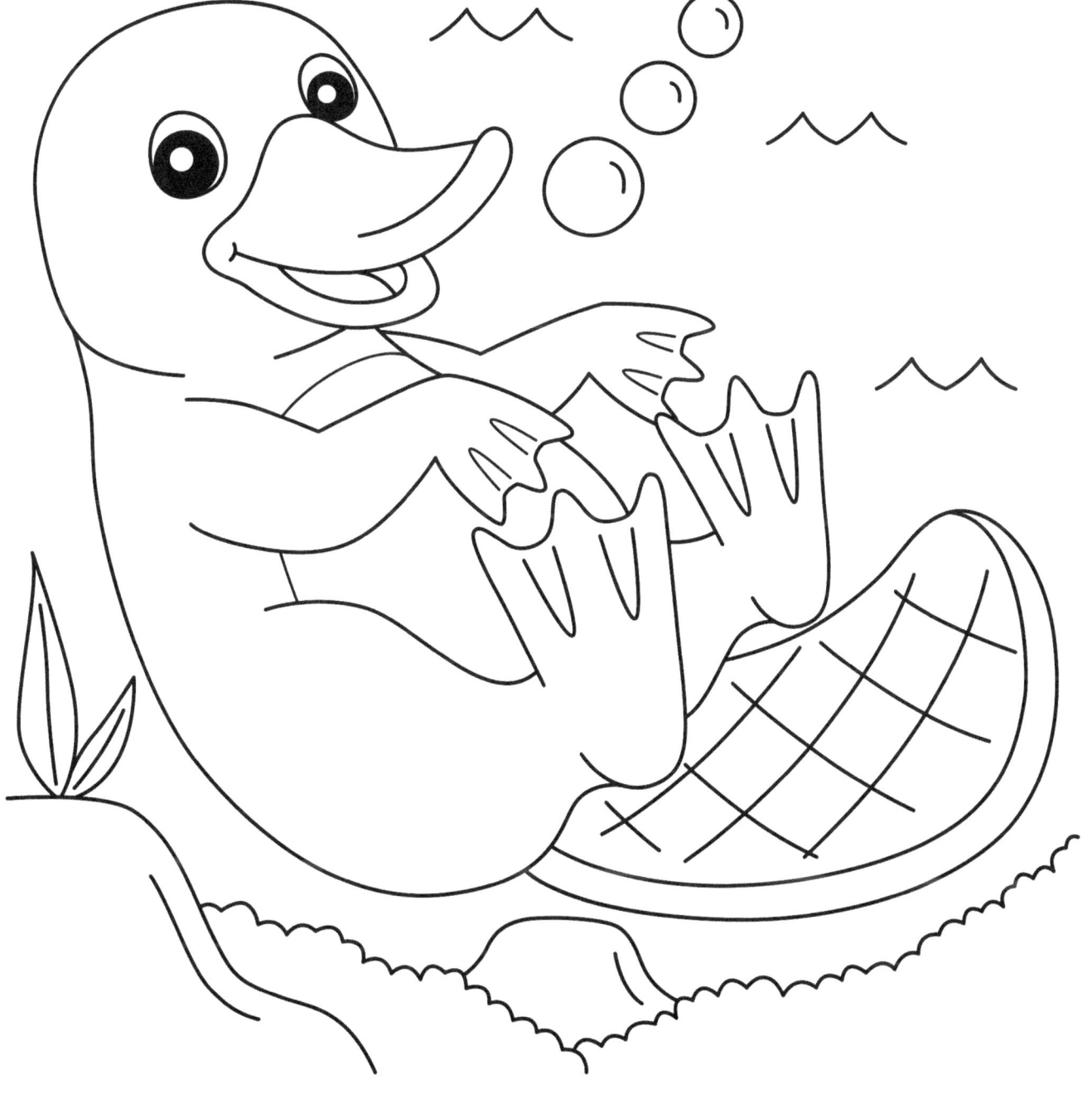

quokka

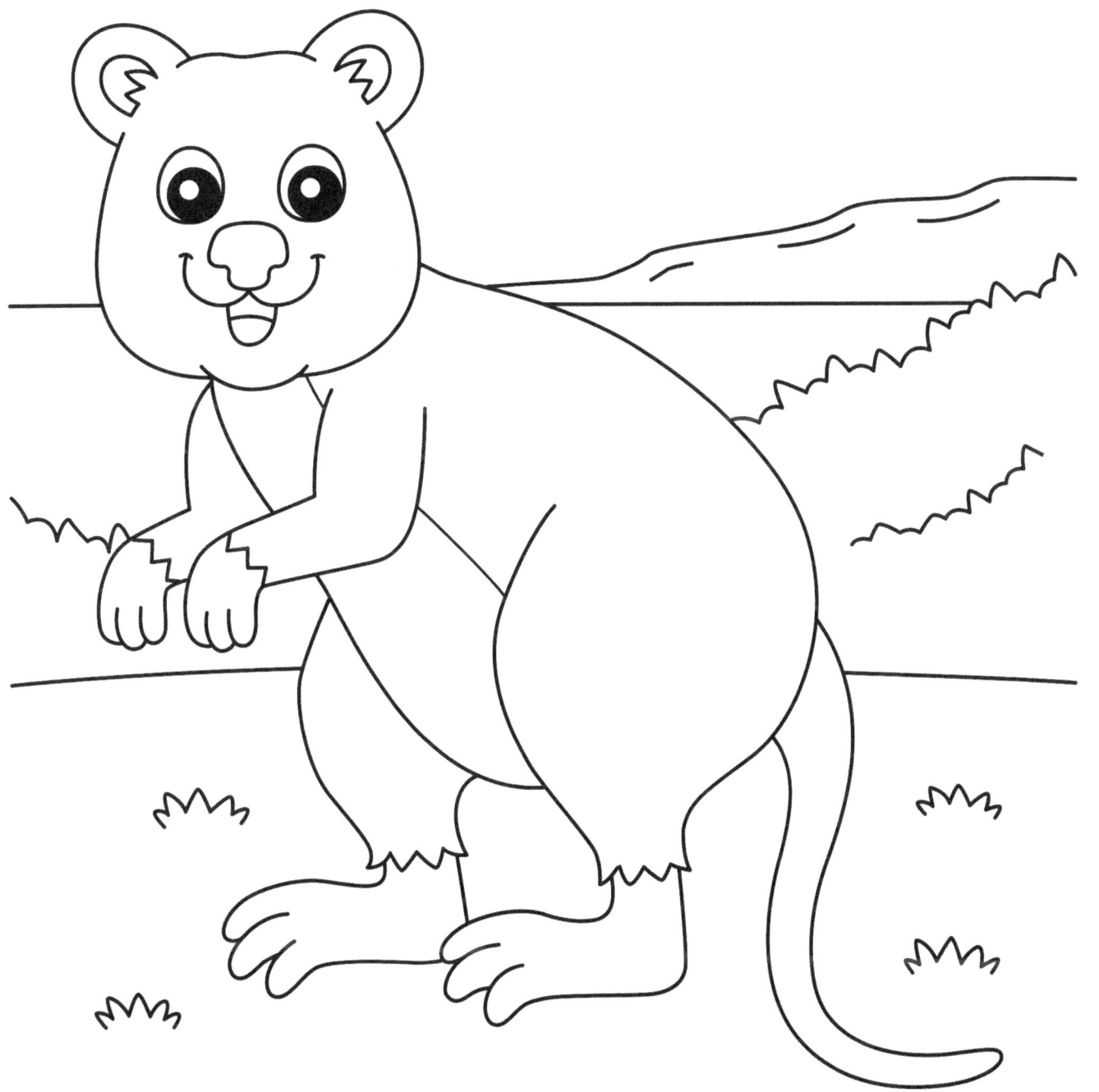

wombat

humpback
whale

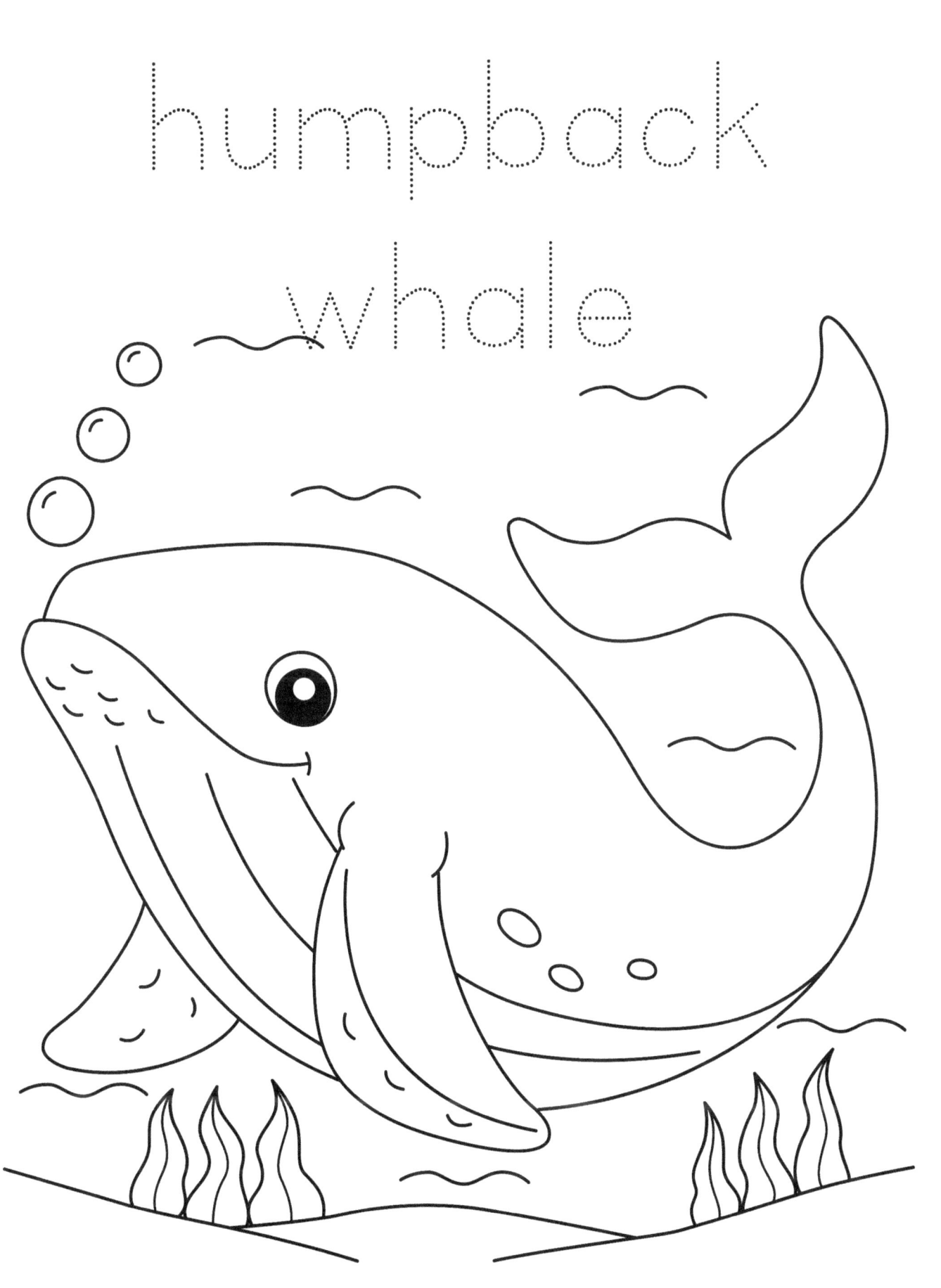

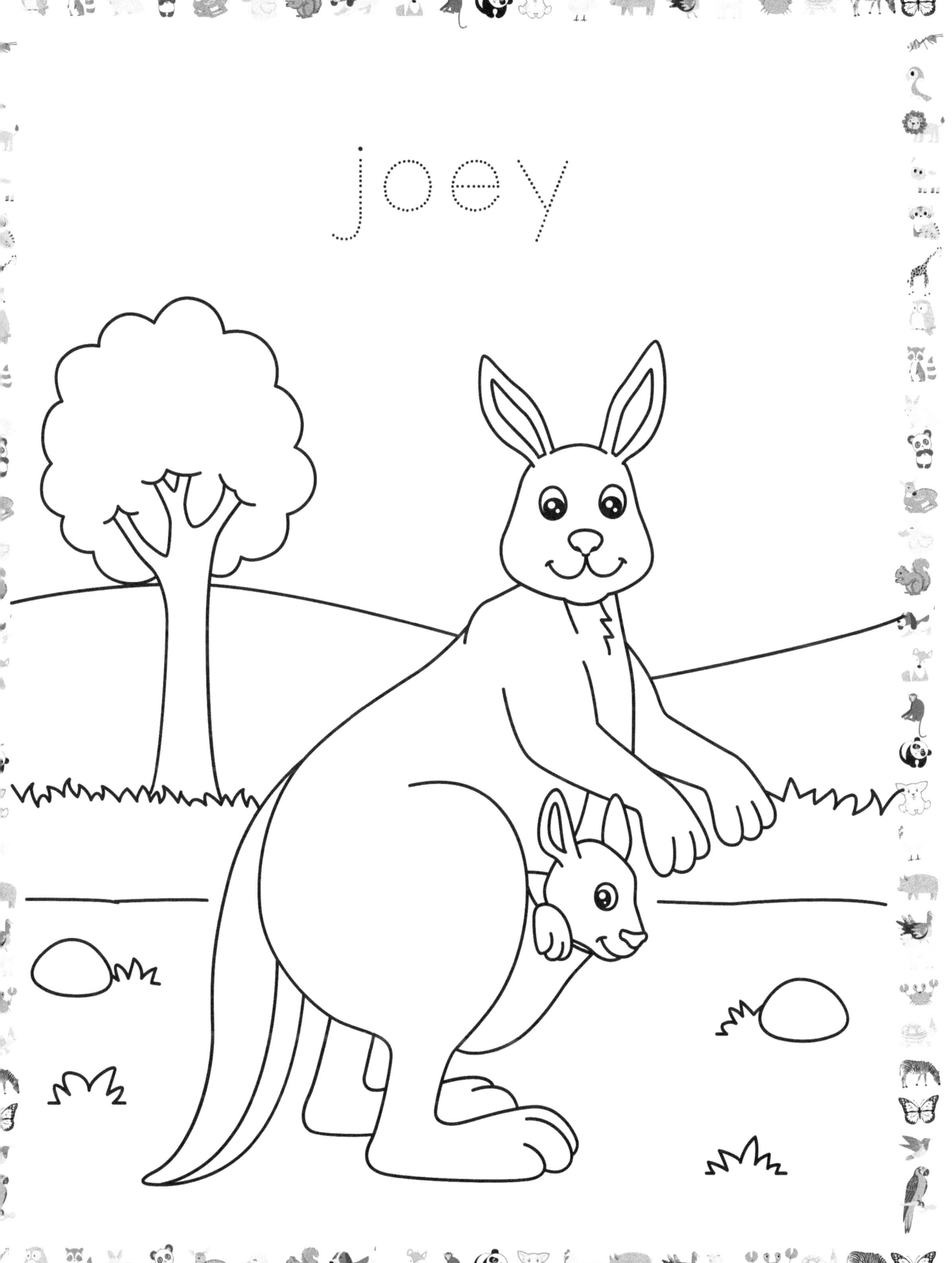

joey

brown
snake

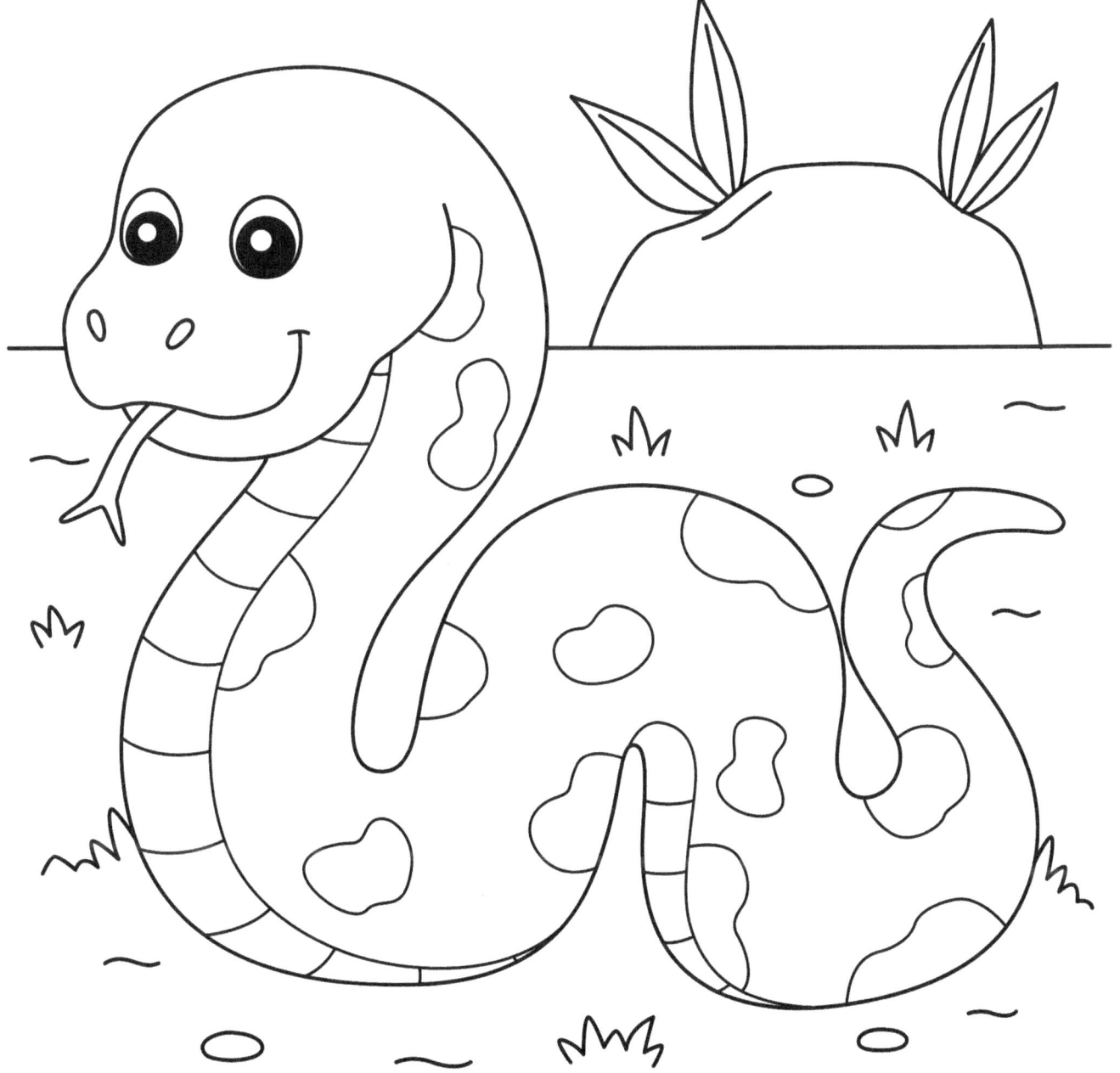

shepherd

dog

bilby

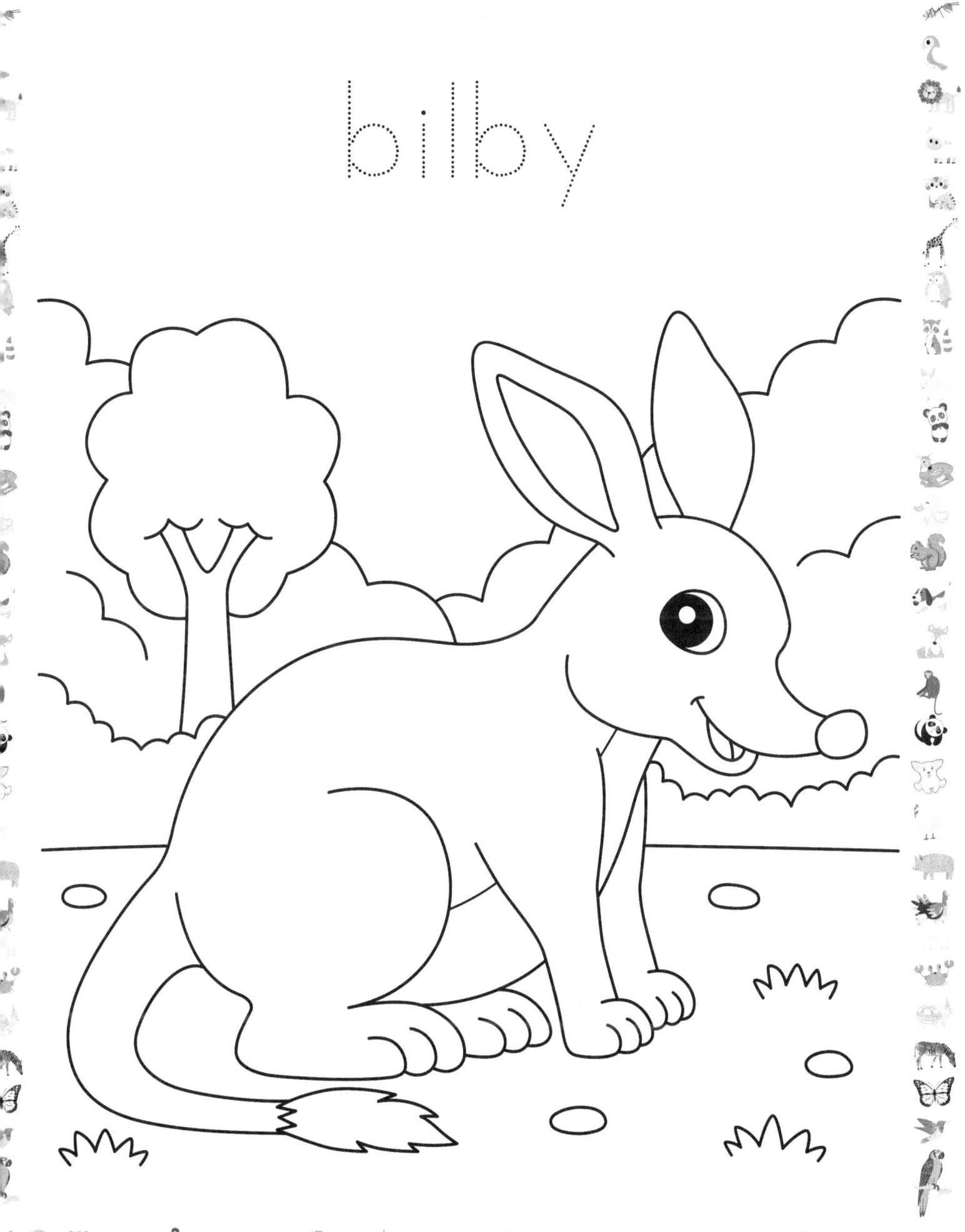

tiger quoll

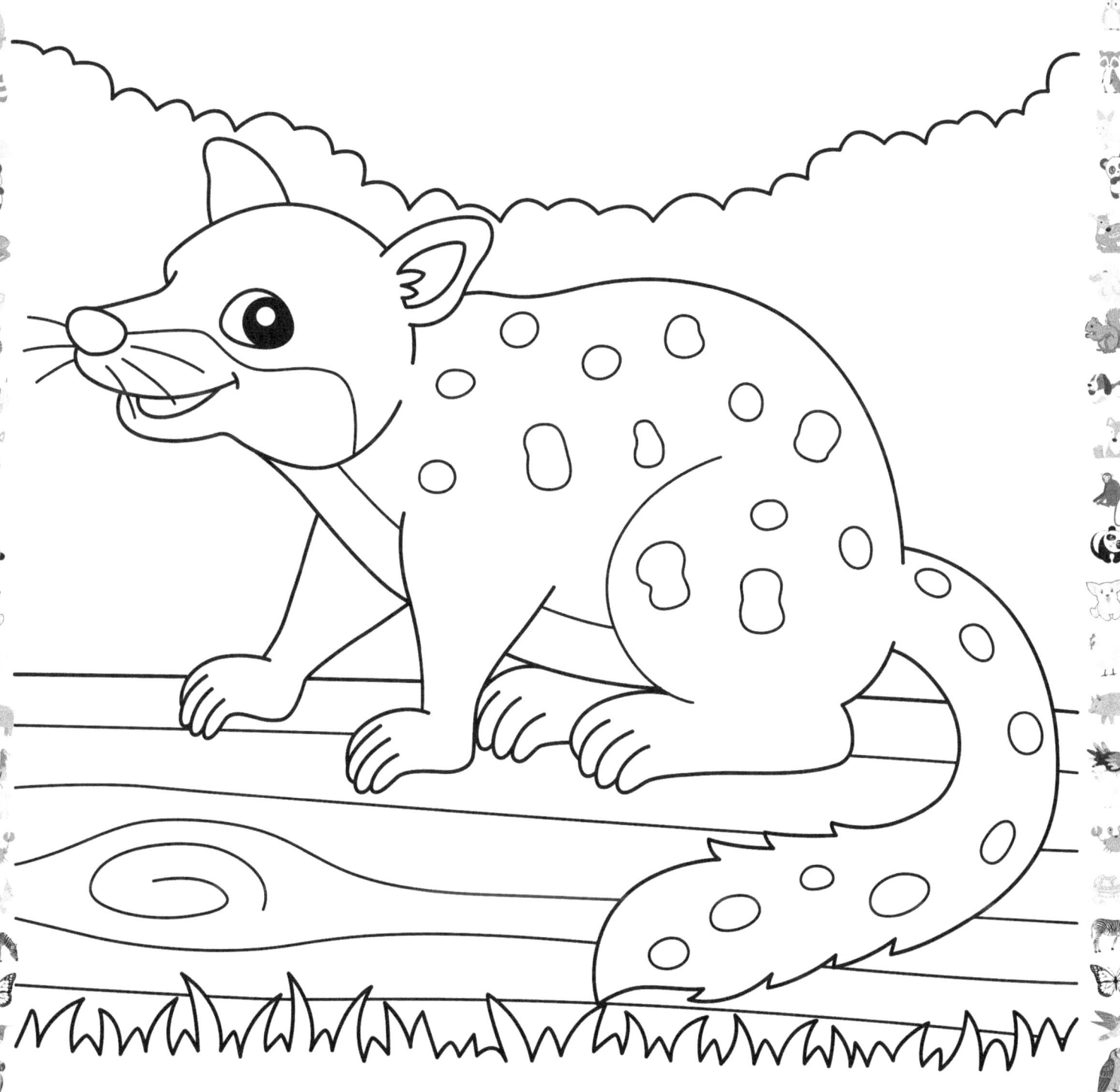

quail

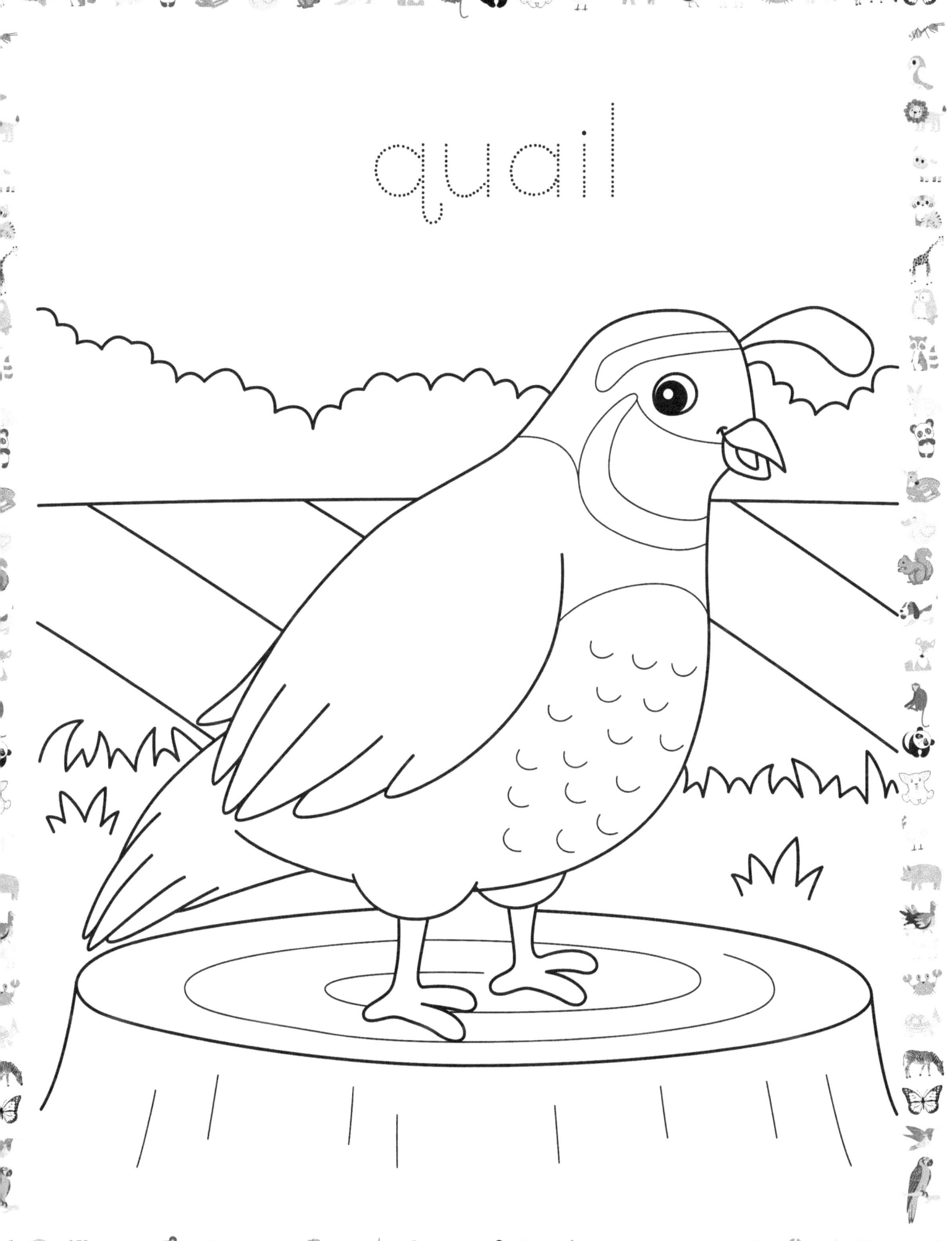

crocodile

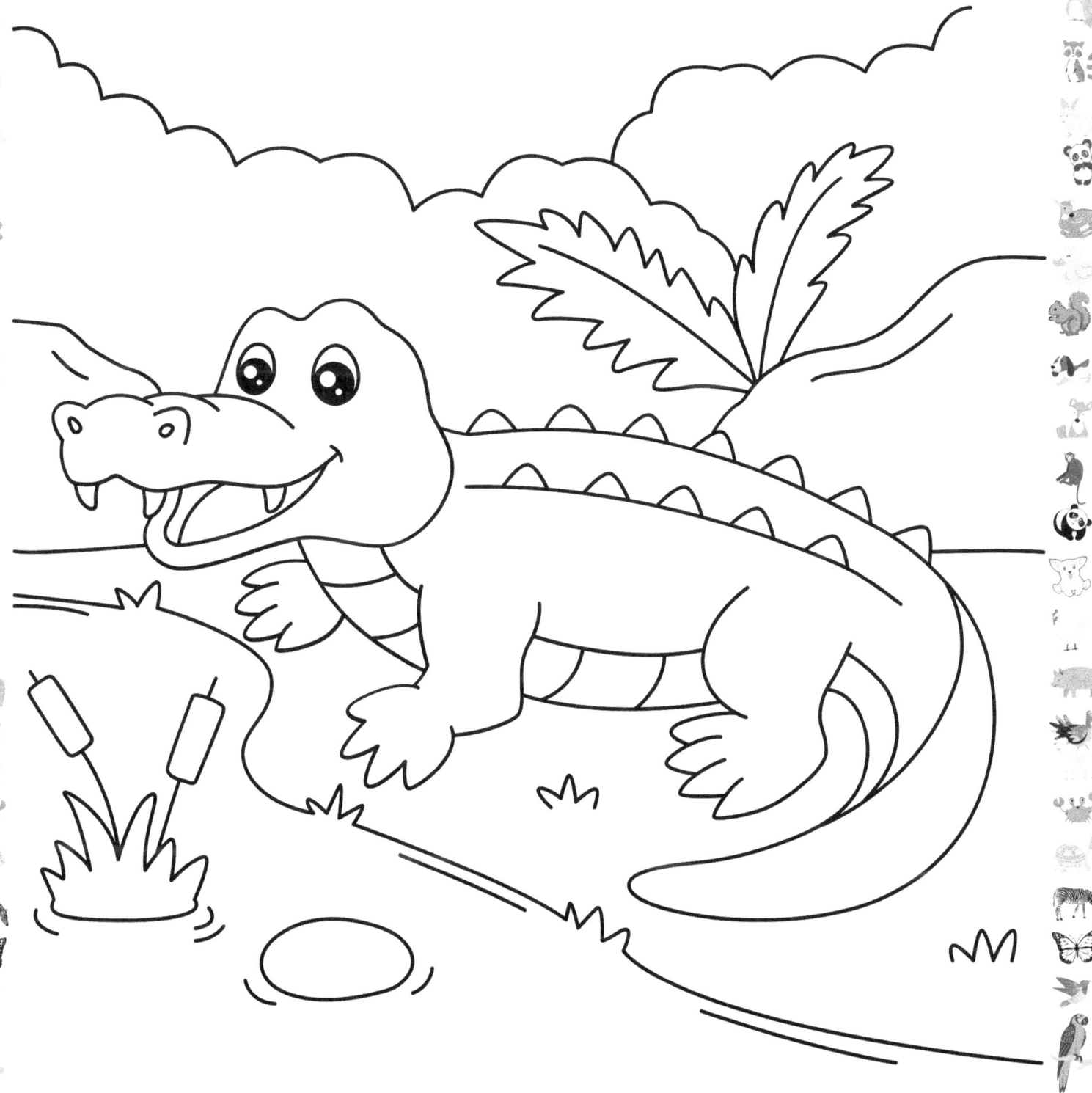

DOG

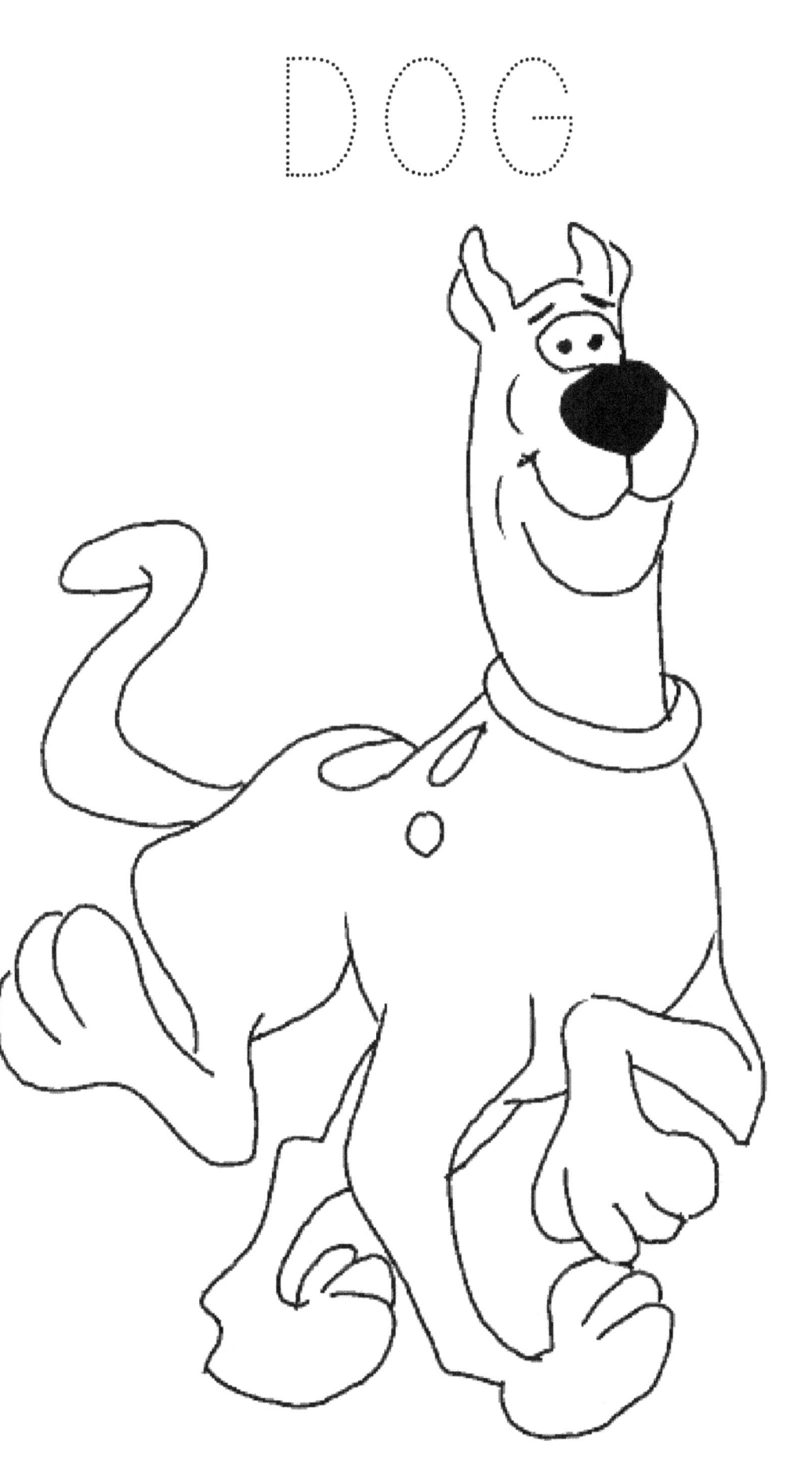

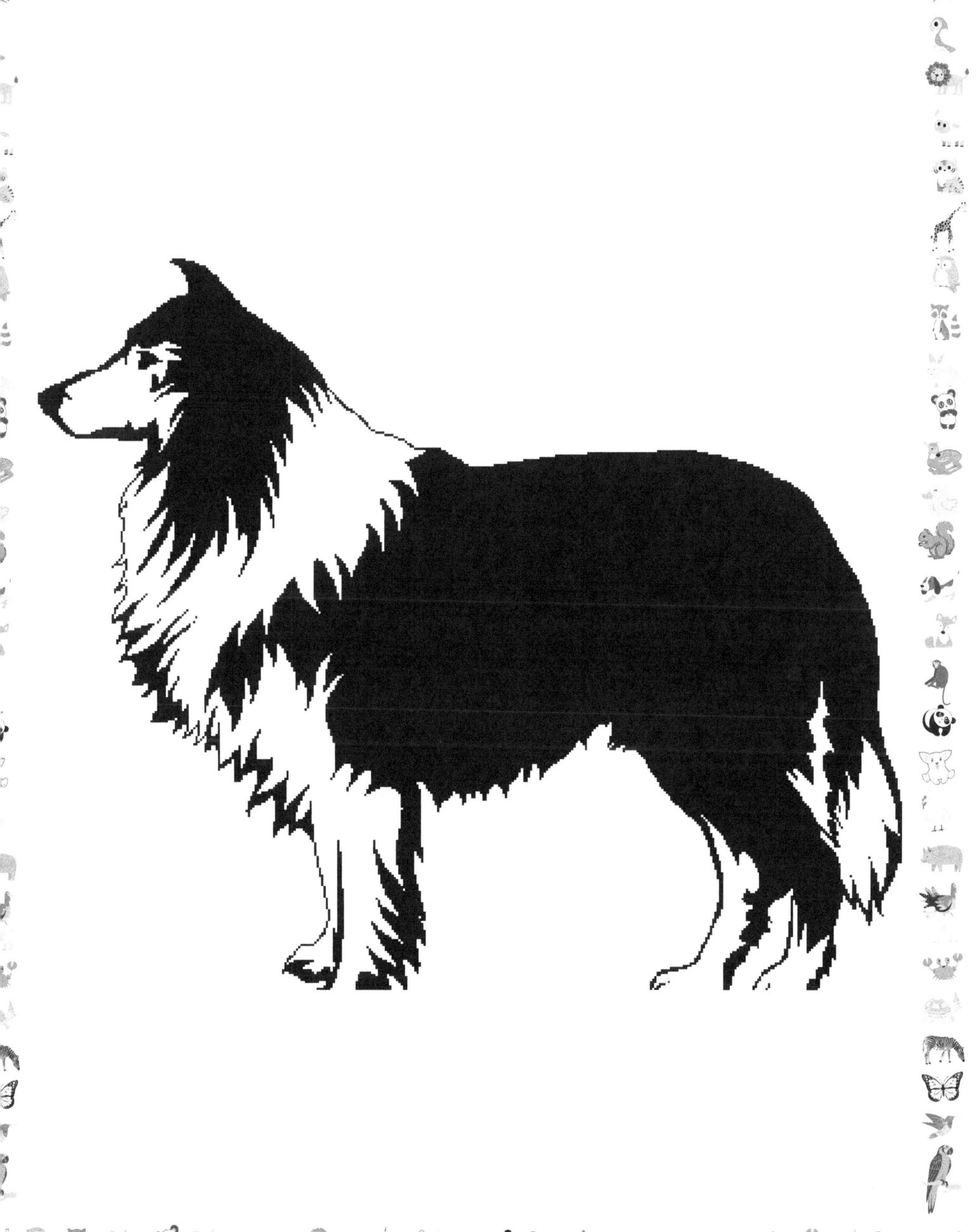

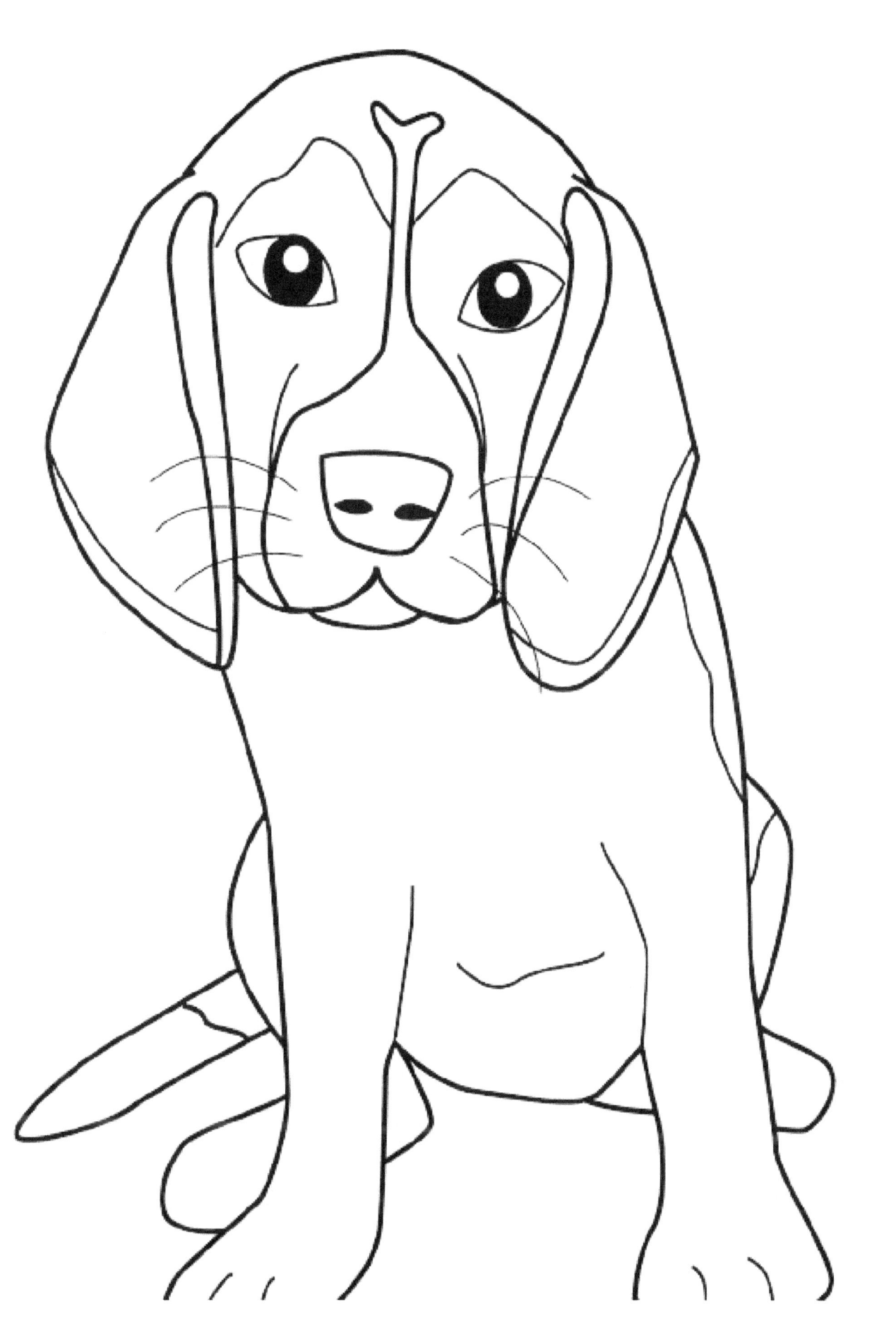

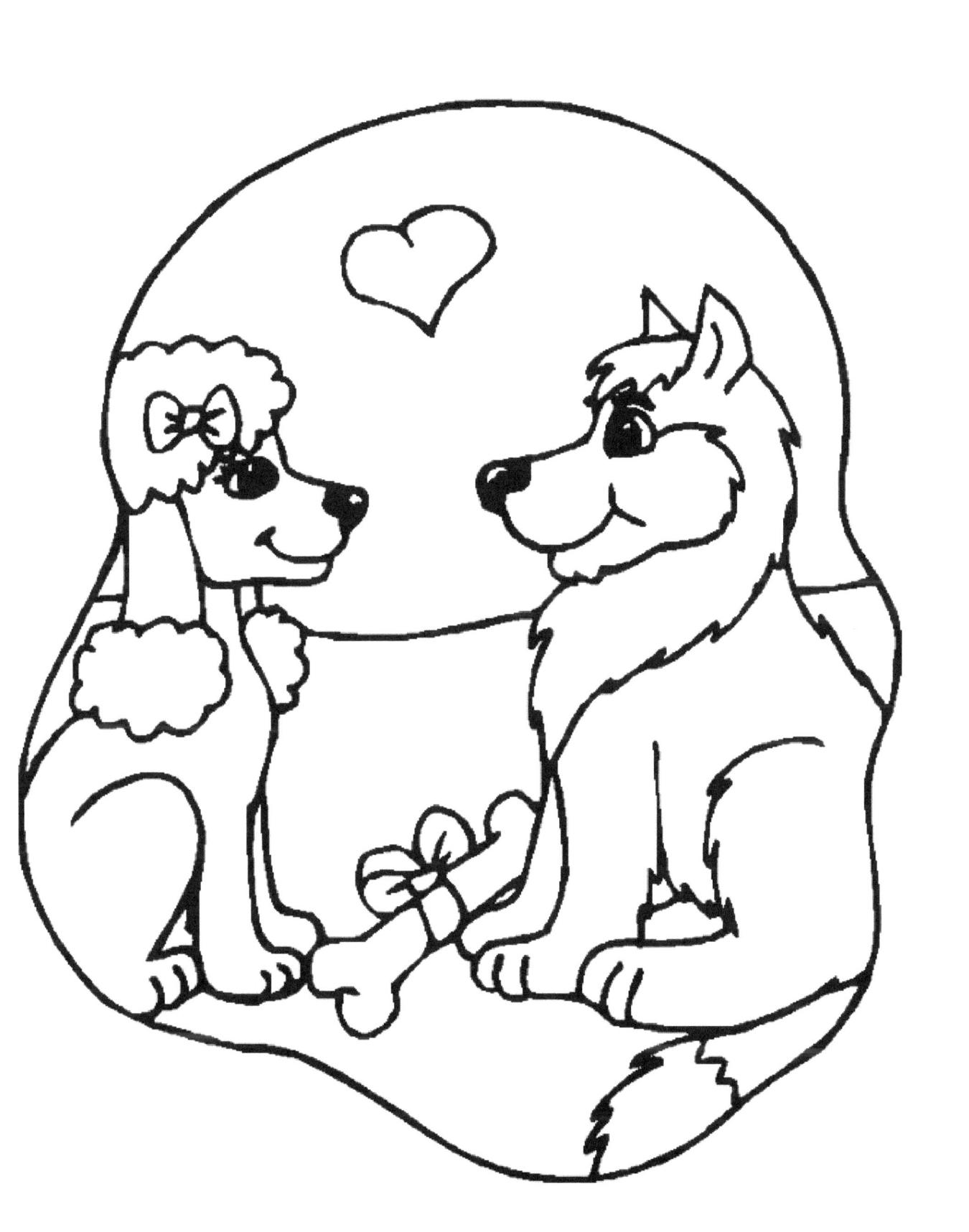

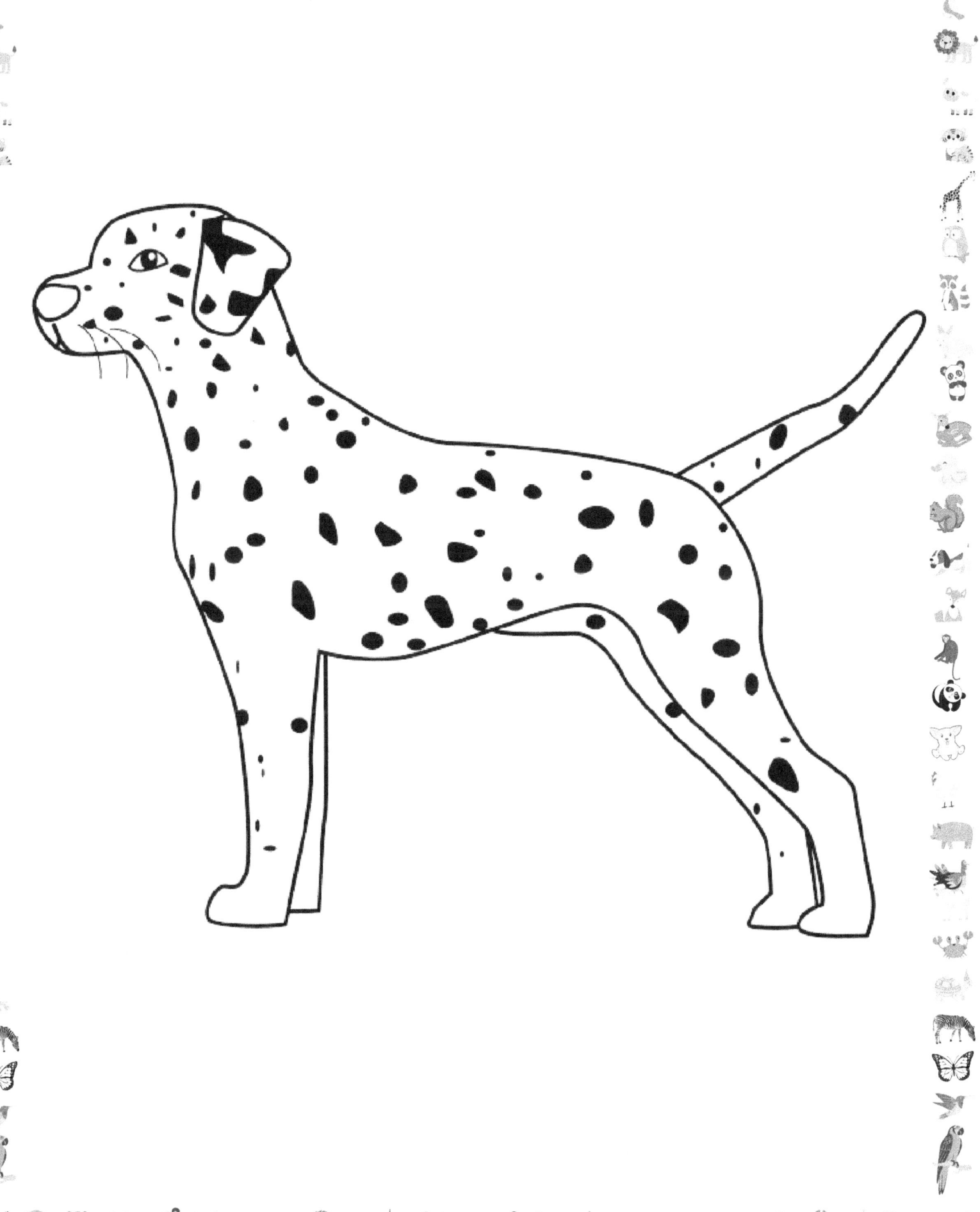

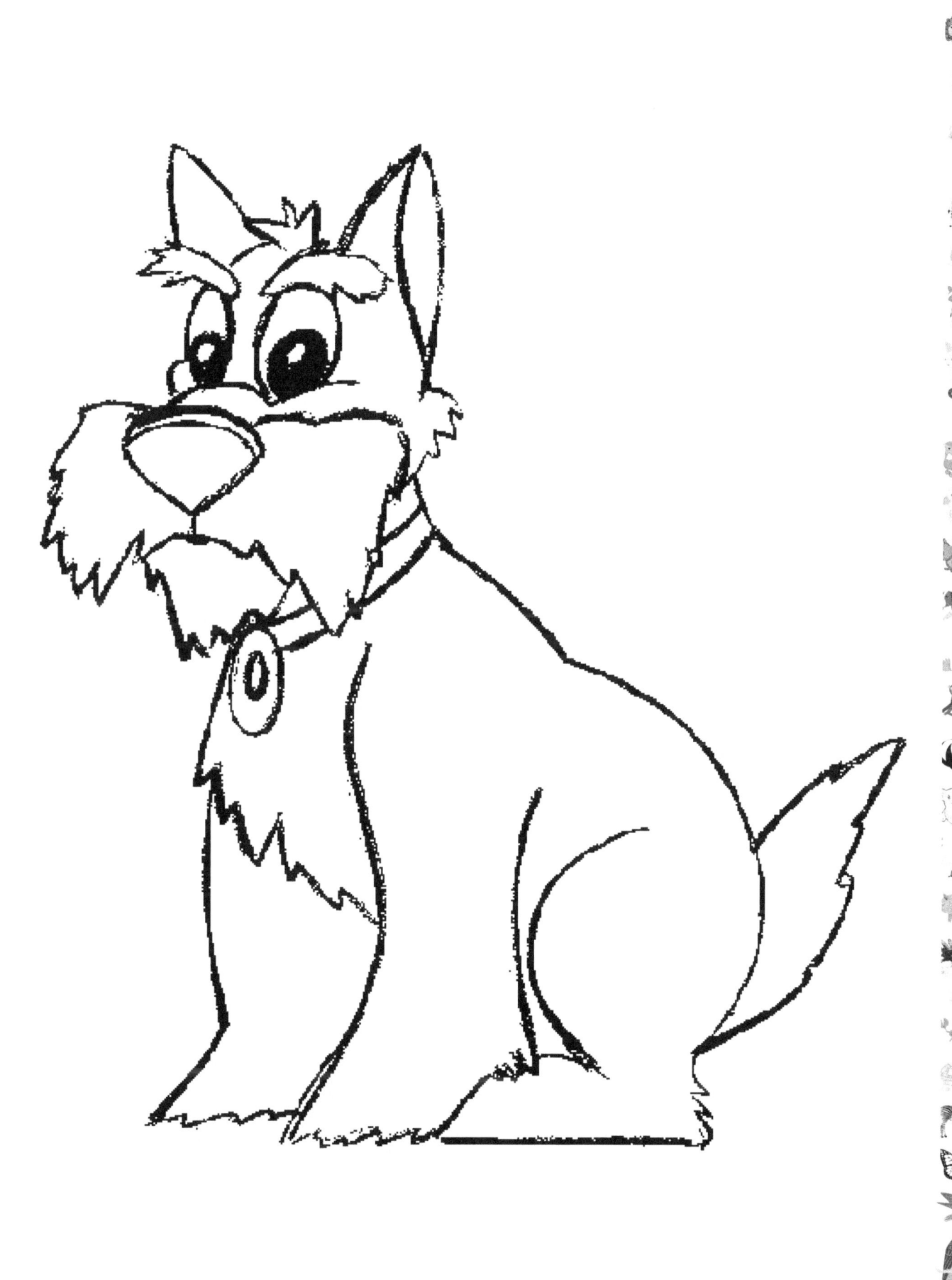

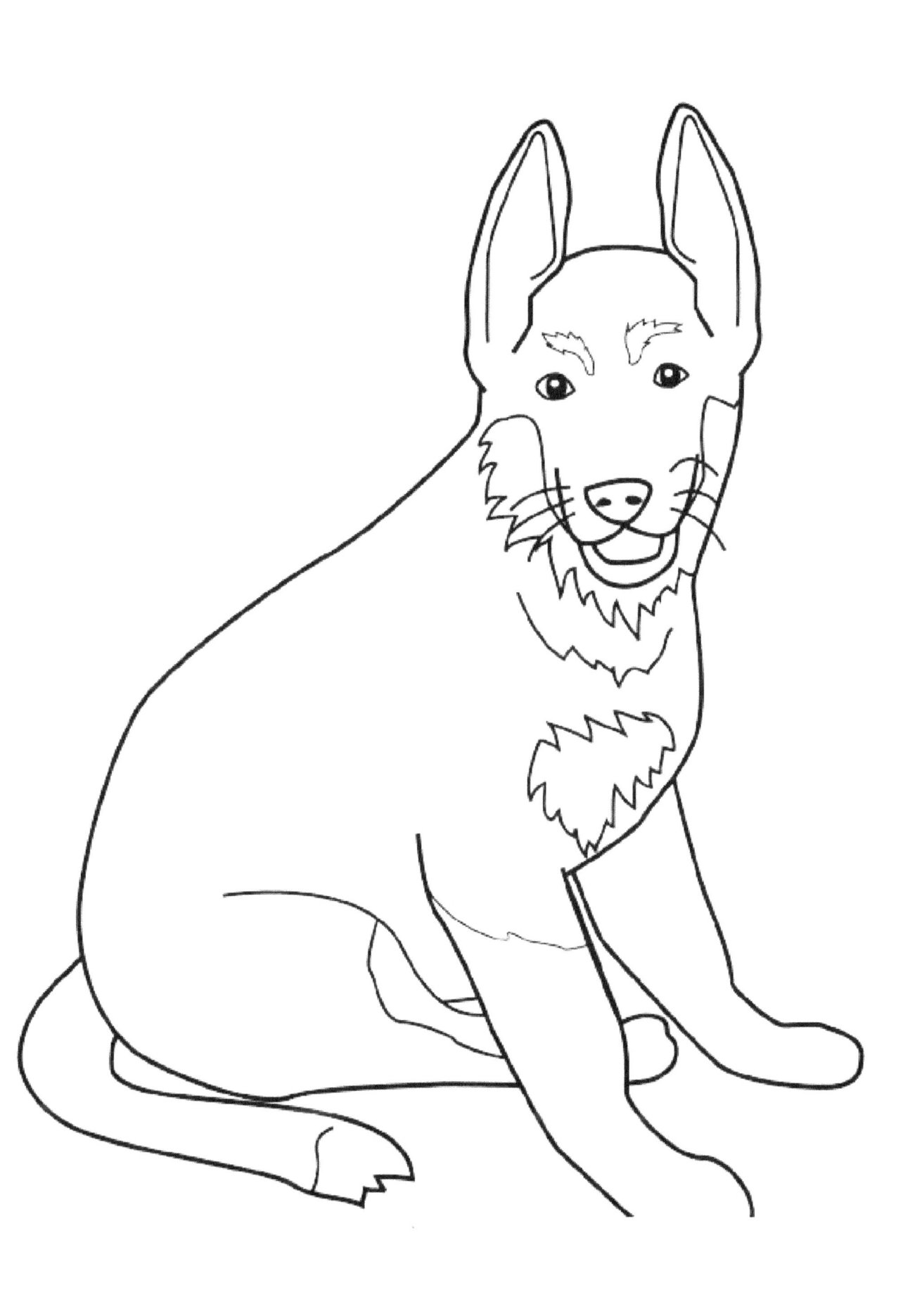

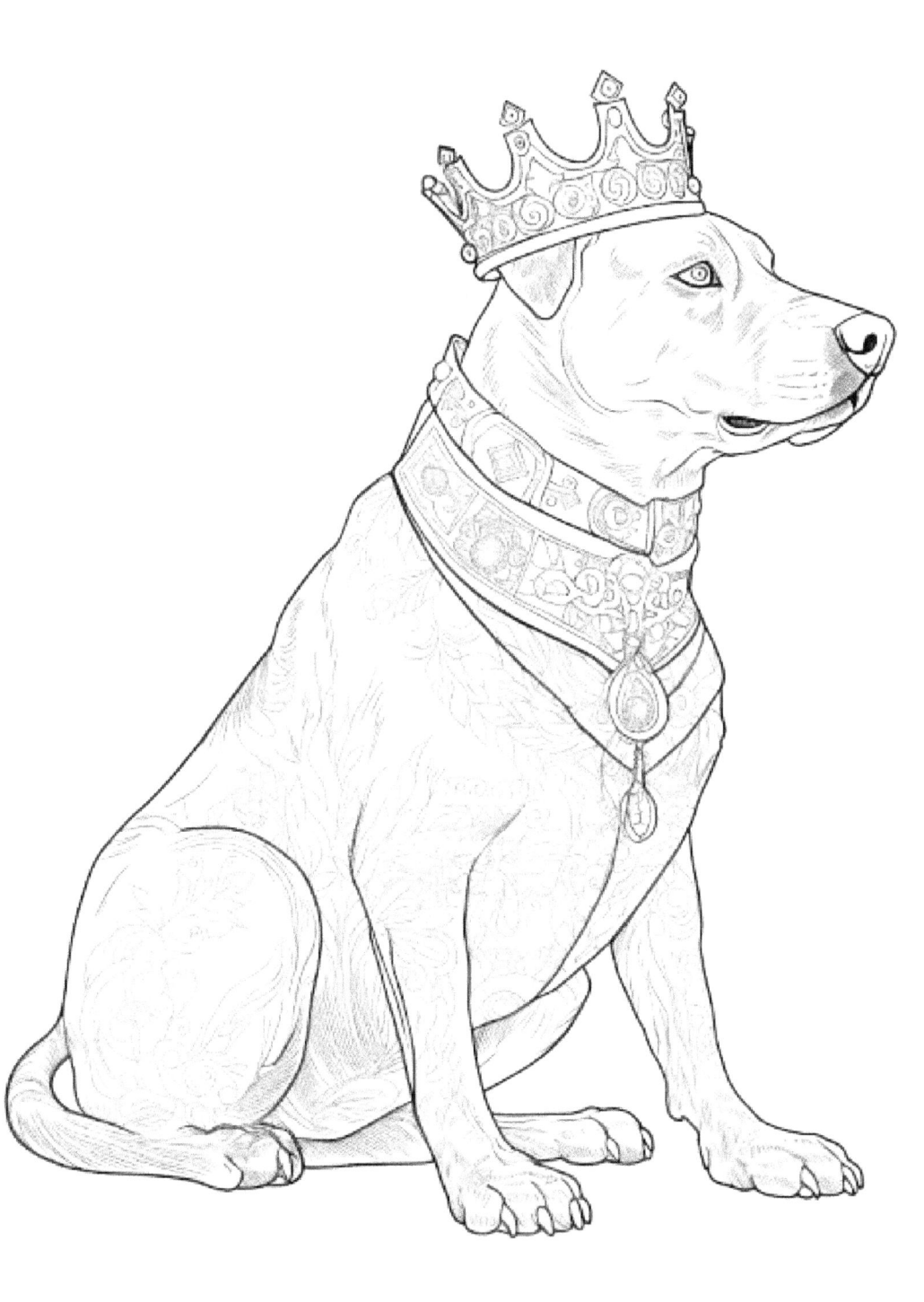

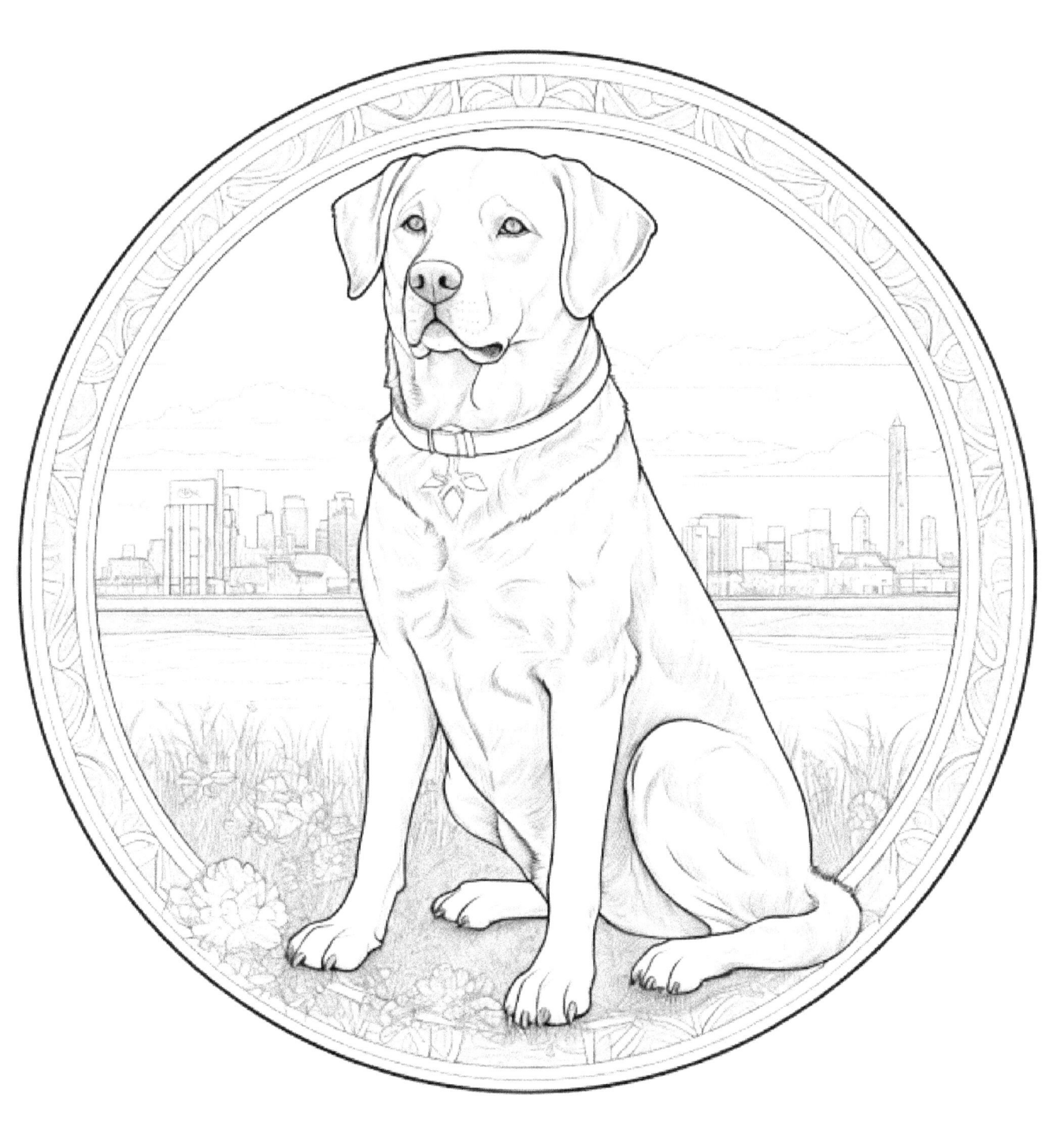

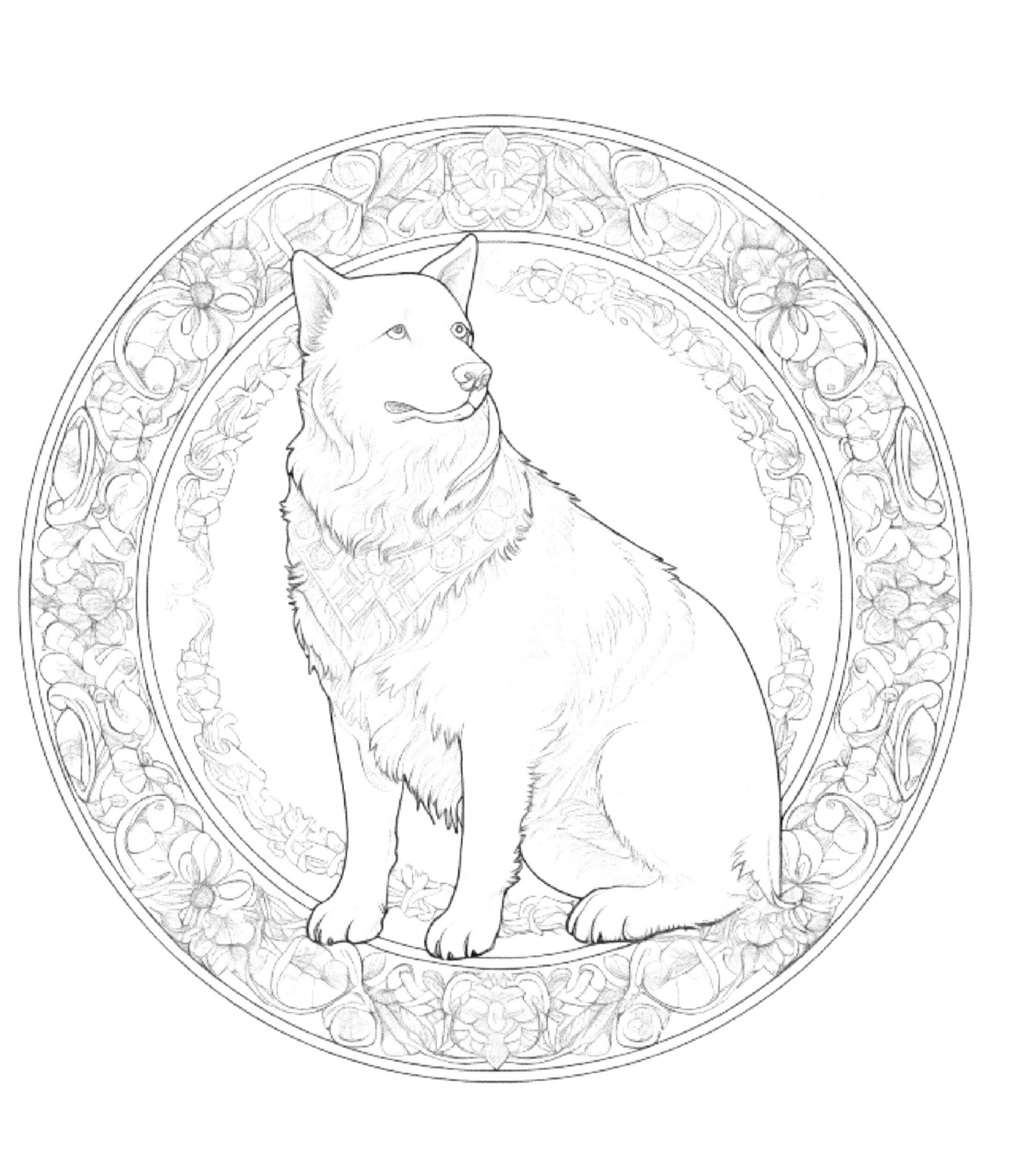

www.ingramcontent.com/pod-product-compliance
Lightning Source LLC
Chambersburg PA
CBHW081450220526
45466CB00008B/2581